# The Rise of Legal Graffiti Writing in New York and Beyond

Ronald Kramer

# The Rise of Legal Graffiti Writing in New York and Beyond

Ronald Kramer
Sociology and Criminology
University of Auckland
Auckland, New Zealand

ISBN 978-981-10-2799-4     ISBN 978-981-10-2800-7 (eBook)
DOI 10.1007/978-981-10-2800-7

Library of Congress Control Number: 2016955178

© The Editor(s) (if applicable) and The Author(s) 2017
This book was advertised with a copyright holder in the name of the publisher in error, whereas the author holds the copyright.
This work is subject to copyright. All rights are solely and exclusively licensed by the Publisher, whether the whole or part of the material is concerned, specifically the rights of translation, reprinting, reuse of illustrations, recitation, broadcasting, reproduction on microfilms or in any other physical way, and transmission or information storage and retrieval, electronic adaptation, computer software, or by similar or dissimilar methodology now known or hereafter developed.
The use of general descriptive names, registered names, trademarks, service marks, etc. in this publication does not imply, even in the absence of a specific statement, that such names are exempt from the relevant protective laws and regulations and therefore free for general use.
The publisher, the authors and the editors are safe to assume that the advice and information in this book are believed to be true and accurate at the date of publication. Neither the publisher nor the authors or the editors give a warranty, express or implied, with respect to the material contained herein or for any errors or omissions that may have been made.

Cover illustration: Abstract Bricks and Shadows © Stephen Bonk/Fotolia.co.uk

Printed on acid-free paper

This Palgrave Macmillan imprint is published by Springer Nature
The registered company is Springer Nature Singapore Pte Ltd.
The registered company address is: 152 Beach Road, #22-06/08 Gateway East, Singapore 189721, Singapore

*For Neera, and Doris, Lee, Sharon, and Glen; and all the stray cats of Brooklyn*

# ACKNOWLEDGMENTS

Durkheim suggested that the religious categories of "good" and "evil" represent the power of society to give life, but to also take it away. An odd example perhaps, the production of a book would seem to verify this sociological insight. One gets to the end of the road and cannot avoid the realization that nothing interesting in life happens without a vast, albeit oftentimes invisible, network of social support.

First and foremost, I would like to thank all the people at Palgrave Macmillan that I have been fortunate enough to work with over the last few months. Special thanks go to Sara Crowley Vigneau for her editorial support. Connie Li and Manoj Mishra, who have worked diligently on countless aspects of this book, also deserve many thanks.

My academic trajectory would not have been possible without the following people: Beryl Langer, who made me realize that being a "stranger in paradise" isn't so bad, Johann Arnason, Joel Kahn, Peter Beilharz, Trevor Hogan, and Rowan Ireland. I also owe an incredible debt to Ronald Eyerman, Rachel Sherman, Jeffrey Alexander, Ivan Szelenyi, Philip Gorski, and Paul Gilroy, who created a supportive environment as a graduate student at Yale University. Also from Yale, Philip Smith has been an ongoing source of support and a well of practical advice that has always been "on point." My colleagues at the University of Auckland—too many to list, but you might be able to find them menus deep on the University of Auckland Web site—have also been supportive since my arrival in 2013. Colleagues with a shared interest in graffiti and street art have been, and remain, incredibly helpful. Along these lines, I owe many thanks to Gregory Snyder, Jeffrey Ian Ross, Joe Austin, Lachlan MacDowall, Pedro Soares Neves, and Daniela Simões.

Many have provided practical forms of support during the research process that went into this book. I am indebted to Paul C. Perkus at the City Hall Library and Leonora Gidlund at the Municipal Archives in New York City. Without their help it is unlikely that I would have been able to find many of the documents upon which much of the analysis came to depend.

I am incredibly grateful for New York City's "graffiti world," especially the writers and "crews" that have welcomed me into their lives over the years. Special thanks go to "Nic One," "Meres," "Demer," "Fargo," "Been3," "Sonic," "Part," "Ema," "Bisc," "MadC," "Cern," "Juse One," "Enz," "Lady Pink," "Too Fly," "Slope MUL," "Cey," "Col," "Break," "Ezo," "Sye," "Veng," "Jean13," "Ree MTA," "Cope2," "Indie184," "Abby," "Riff," "DJ Charm," "Sue," "Bader," "Dezo," "Wane," and "Skore"—the list just goes on and on. Also from the graffiti world, a special "shout out" goes to "Pase," "Jew," "Abe," and all the other Bronx Team writers. The "BT Lab" was certainly a highlight of life in New York.

Those who spend countless hours documenting graffiti deserve special mention. It is great to see all the graffiti enthusiasts who have entered the picture in recent times. I know there are quite a few, but I would especially like to thank "Luna Park" and Roman Akkerman (AKA "Photograffiti by Roman").

It almost goes without saying, but I owe many thanks to my immediate family, Doris, Lee, Sharon, and Glen.

Finally, a very special thank you goes out to Neera Jain. A state-sanctioned "partner in crime" since 2008, she somehow puts up with my raccoon-like and aspergian ways. One day we will have five cats that determine all of our interior design decisions.

## Permissions Page

Chapters 3, 5, and 6 incorporate some material from the following journal articles:

Kramer, R. "Political Elites, 'Broken Windows,' and the Commodification of Urban Space." *Critical Criminology* 20, no. 3 (2012): 229–248.

Kramer, R. "Painting with Permission: Legal Graffiti in New York City." *Ethnography* 11, no. 2 (2010): 235–253.

Kramer, R. "Moral Panics and Urban Growth Machines: Official Reactions to Graffiti in New York City, 1990–2005." *Qualitative Sociology* 33, no. 3 (2010): 297–311.

The respective copyright holders have graciously allowed that portions of these articles be republished here.

# Contents

1 Introduction   1

2 The Extraction of Subway Graffiti: The Late 1960s to 1989   9

3 The "Clean Train" Era: Creating a Space for the Legal Production of Graffiti   35

4 Responding to the New Graffiti Writing Culture: Broader Publics, Art Worlds, and the Sphere of Commodity Exchange   61

5 The Moral Panic over Graffiti in New York City: Political Elites and the Mass Print Media   83

6 Engendering Desire for Neoliberal Penality and the Logic of Growth Machines   103

7 Conclusion   127

Appendix   133

Bibliography   141

Index   155

# LIST OF FIGURES

| | | |
|---|---|---|
| Fig. 2.1 | An example of an early tag by "Cornbread." Photo by Ramon Been3 Vasquez | 13 |
| Fig. 2.2 | An example of a "straight letter" piece by "Wane," which incorporates the "cast shadow" effect | 14 |
| Fig. 2.3 | An example of a "wildstyle" piece by "Logek." Note the "flat 3D" effect | 15 |
| Fig. 2.4 | Four types of design features within letters | 16 |
| Fig. 2.5 | A piece by "Kezam" that embodies the "real 3D" letterform | 17 |
| Fig. 2.6 | Painted by "Nme," a piece with cloud/background | 18 |
| Fig. 2.7 | A "throw-up" by "Baby 168" | 18 |
| Fig. 2.8 | "Scratchiti" and "etch" bombing | 28 |
| Fig. 3.1 | A "rollie piece" painted by "Smells" and "Cash4" from a building rooftop | 45 |
| Fig. 3.2 | An example of a "production" featuring work by "Tone," "Hef," "KA," and "Yes1" | 50 |
| Fig. 3.3 | A second example of a "production" painted by "Pase," "Welin," and "Me3" | 50 |

CHAPTER 1

# Introduction

**Abstract** The introduction situates *The Rise of Legal Graffiti in New York and Beyond* in relation to previous scholarship on graffiti. Whereas this scholarship tends to emphasize graffiti as an illegal practice with an accompanying political ethos of "resistance," this book promises a discussion of how graffiti writing changed after 1989 and how this led to new subcultural worldviews and practices. The introduction summarizes the structure of the book by outlining the key claims in each substantive chapter.

**Keywords** Graffiti · Aesthetics · New York City · Neoliberalism · Urban growth · Ethnography · Subculture

In the late 1960s, a new approach to writing graffiti, set apart by emphasizing an individual name through aesthetic stylization, emerged within northeastern US cities. This new type of public writing has been absorbed by academic discourse in several ways. On the one hand, there is a tendency to treat graffiti writing culture as a fragmentary piece within broader (youth) cultural formations. In these cases, graffiti is seen as an "element" of "hip-hop" or as a variation on gang markings.[1] On the other

---

[1] Chang, *Can't Stop Won't Stop* (2005); Hager, *Hip Hop* (1984); Phillips, *Wallbangin'* (1999); Rose, *Black Noise* (1994).

© The Author(s) 2017
R. Kramer, *The Rise of Legal Graffiti Writing in New York and Beyond*, DOI 10.1007/978-981-10-2800-7_1

hand, some scholars perceive graffiti writing culture as something that warrants study in its own right. While this approach is certainly more desirable, it suffers from a number of limitations. Most notably, such accounts tend to focus on graffiti as it existed in New York City throughout the 1970s and the 1980s, a time during which it was practiced, for the most part, illegally on subway trains. Alternatively, scholars focus on emergent graffiti writing cultures in other parts of the world, or in other US cities, that took their inspiration from what was happening in New York City. Once again, the focus here has overwhelmingly been placed on graffiti writing as an illegal practice.[2]

Alongside the emphasis on illegality, there has been an ongoing attempt to discover the meaning of graffiti. By accepting the notion that graffiti generally takes place somewhere beyond accepted boundaries of social and cultural normality and, of course, legality, the meaning of graffiti often ends up being painted with fairly predictable brushstrokes, even by the most sympathetic of observers. In most accounts, graffiti figures as a site of "resistance." Exactly what is being resisted varies by author. For Ferrell, it is an authoritarian order that, insofar as this is embedded within the physical urban environment, is rightfully challenged; in Miller's account, it is consumer society alongside class and "race" contradictions that comes under attack; for Rahn, it is regulatory discourses that shape the movement from adolescence to adulthood that are negotiated by graffiti writing. In other accounts, such as Macdonald's, graffiti is posited not so much as an arena of resistance, but one of hostility and lashing out against society. Despite their differences, to the extent that they portray the relationship between graffiti and society as one marked by discordance, these interpretations have much in common not only with one another, but also with the dominant discourse on graffiti, which tends to see it as an external threat to social order.[3]

Although less explored in the academic discourse, attempts to address the problem of how and why various sectors of society (such as the political elite) react to graffiti have been colored by the tendency to see graffiti writers as occupying an "outsider" status. If graffiti resists an authoritarian order, as in Ferrell's account, then it follows that opposition to graffiti

---

[2] Austin, *Taking the Train* (2001); Ferrell, *Crimes of Style* (1993); Lachmann, "Graffiti as Career" (1988); Macdonald, *Graffiti Subculture* (2001); Miller, *Aerosol Kingdom* (2002); Rahn, *Painting without Permission* (2002).

[3] Kramer, "Moral Panics and Urban Growth" (2010).

represents an attempt to maintain or reestablish that order, to reproduce a society hierarchically organized along dimensions of class, gender, "race," and so on. Roughly following a Marxist approach, Austin has argued that New York City's official reaction to graffiti throughout the 1970s and the 1980s was based on the need to create a scapegoat group and social problem that could be blamed for the civic collapse that followed a period of economic mismanagement and crisis.[4]

In short, working within specific times and spaces, previous literature has tended to take the illegality of graffiti for granted. Moreover, it is on this basis that subsequent ideas concerning the meaning of graffiti, and official responses to it, have been developed and bequeathed to us. Although the spatial focus on New York City is not new, this book traces a very different historical moment of graffiti writing culture. As a result, it reaches very different conclusions concerning the nature of graffiti writing and the reasons that undergird official responses to the practice.

## NEW YORK CITY GRAFFITI AFTER 1989

As is well known among graffiti writers, and those with an interest in graffiti writing culture, 1989 marks a major turning point, a fundamental rupture with the past. It was in the middle of that year that the subway system was declared to be "graffiti free."[5] This put an end to a 20-year history during which the aesthetic and cultural values of graffiti writing were crystallized and initially developed. Among political elites, this accomplishment was celebrated as a major victory over an apparent scourge of the city. Among intellectuals with an eye looking in this direction, it would appear that 1989 has been accepted, albeit very implicitly, as a moment that marks the end of graffiti as a historical thread; as if it were an aesthetic trajectory truncated by state power. However, what happened to graffiti writing culture after 1989 not only forces us to rethink the significance of the 1970s and the 1980s, but also the nature of graffiti writing and the reasons that drive officials to oppose it as vehemently as they do.

In what follows, I make three interrelated arguments. First, with hindsight, we can understand the 1970s and the 1980s as representing a time

---

[4] Ferrell, *Crimes of Style* (1993); Austin, *Taking the Train* (2001).
[5] Schmidlapp and Phase2, *Style Writing* (1996).

period in which history was occurring behind the backs of its major actors. Far from suppressing anything, state policies, noteworthy for their unquenchable desire to eradicate graffiti, simply squeezed it out of the subway system and compelled it to find new urban spaces in which to thrive.

Second, one of the major outcomes of this was the emergence of legal graffiti. Among subway painters of the 1970s and the 1980s, a significant portion were committed to producing elaborate murals on the sides of subway cars. These graffiti writers would spend prolonged periods of time in yards and lay-ups producing detailed work. But with the state blocking entrance to the subway system as a place to paint, this group of writers had a hard time finding an acceptable substitute "above ground." As such, they started seeking out permission from property owners to produce graffiti. With the turn to legal graffiti, a new ethos among many writers has developed. Not only do they tend to lead conventional lives and subscribe to conventional values, they also seek to find a place within society. Far from "resisting," many *wish* to be coopted by society in order to attain the privileges and benefits, especially monetary rewards, that it is capable of offering.

Third, given this state of affairs, the official reaction to graffiti in New York City can be understood in a very new way, one that will bring us into contact with some additional bodies of academic literature. The most salient aspect to note concerning the official reaction to graffiti is its persistence over time, and this *despite major changes in the nature of graffiti writing*. For the last 40 or so years, the city has vehemently clung to the notions that graffiti is illegal, bad, a serious urban problem that threatens everybody in one way or another. It is now readily apparent that such a discourse is profoundly out of step with historical reality. Insofar as the official reaction to graffiti consists of exaggerated claims concerning its social and economic impact, it makes sense to theorize antigraffiti rhetoric and practice as a moral panic, which can be understood as an overreaction to a phenomenon that is relatively inconsequential.[6] With sociologists offering strikingly dissimilar explanations for moral panics, the literature on the topic is quite diverse. Those following Durkheim have suggested that panics articulate and reinscribe the social norms that hold a society together. Marxists have tended to understand

---

[6] Cohen, *Folk Devils* (1972); Goode and Ben-Yehuda, *Moral Panics* (1994).

panics as diversions that are trotted out in times of economic crisis to deflect attention away from capitalist class relations. Those following Foucault's ideas about knowledge and biopower have tended to understand them as ideological maneuvers that promulgate norms that regulate the human body or populations.[7]

Inspired by a variety of critical scholarship, the chapters that follow develop a new perspective on moral panics. I situate the moral panic over graffiti in relation to two broad structural dynamics that characterize late capitalist societies: neoliberal state-crafting and the commodification of urban space. Neoliberal state-crafting can be understood as a social formation marked by growing inequality, combined with an expansive criminal justice system, that seeks to manage the most vulnerable and marginalized through punitive means.[8] In this context, political elites exploit graffiti writing culture in ways that facilitate the normalization of the punitive tendencies inherent to neoliberalism.

The relationship between urban commodification and moral panics over graffiti can be established by demonstrating how the city's antigraffiti standpoint mirrors the ideology of privatism and dovetails with the interests of growth machines. The ideology of privatism and growth machines are two concepts of central importance among scholars interested in understanding how cities develop their particular social, cultural, and economic contours. "Privatism" is perhaps best understood as an ideology that adapts the basic principles of neoliberal economics to the urban context. It essentially claims that the city (i.e., the state) should do everything in its power to facilitate the functioning of capitalist interests and needs. In relation to the urban realm, this means that the city should strive to create a climate that is "business-friendly" and geared toward rising property values.[9]

To say that this is an ideology is to intimate that it is not simply a free-floating discourse, but is tied to a set of material practices and projects. Following Logan and Molotch, the physical counterpart to privatism can

---

[7] For the Durkheimian model, see Erikson, *Wayward Puritans* (1966); for the Marxist approach, see Hall et al., *Policing the Crisis* (1978); Watney, *Policing Desire* (1987), follows Foucault.
[8] Wacquant, *Prisons of Poverty* (2009a).
[9] Logan and Molotch, *Urban Fortunes* (1987); Smith, *New Urban Frontier* (1996); Squires, "Partnership" (2011).

be understood as the "growth machine." Growth machines are loose coalitions that form between local political leaders, landowners, corporate developers, and speculators. What unites these agents is a shared interest in extracting the maximum profit possible from how urban space is put to use and, more or less simultaneously, a basic disregard for meeting the relatively modest needs of most people or city residents.[10]

The correspondence between these concepts and opposition to graffiti, I will suggest, becomes clear when we look at statements made within the mass print media and by public officials as they go about articulating their antigraffiti standpoint. Spelling out these links amounts to claiming that the city's antigraffiti rhetoric and practice is governed by a disposition that understands urban space as akin to a commodity, one that, like any other commodity, ought to be manufactured and consumed solely for the sake of profit, even if this demands sacrificing "use value." That is to say, at the root of the city's antigraffiti efforts one discovers the political and economic imperative to manufacture a social and urban environment that caters, more or less exclusively, to the consumption abilities and habits of society's wealthier classes, and this at the expense of those who are socially disadvantaged.

## THE STRUCTURE OF THE BOOK

The chapters in this book build upon one another to elucidate these central arguments. Utilizing the work of earlier scholars, Chap. 2 synthesizes the first two decades—1970–1989—of graffiti writing's history in New York City. I begin by exploring the development of graffiti as an aesthetic practice and then consider how the city, art worlds, and cultural media responded to this new public phenomenon. However, instead of attempting to explain the origins of graffiti, and rather than seeking to identify the dynamics behind the social responses to it, this recasting of history has a different purpose. In exploring the 1970s and the 1980s, what I wish to suggest is that all of the major actors in question—the writers, the city, art worlds, cultural media—were engaging in behaviors the consequences of which they could not, and did not, foresee. What was effectively happening from the early 1970s through to the end of 1989 was a relocating of graffiti, a forced migration, which saw it move out of

---

[10] Logan and Molotch, *Urban Fortunes* (1987).

the subway system only to take up residence "above ground." This is particularly paradoxical given all of the city's antigraffiti efforts: while it would not be untrue to say that state policies did put an end to publicly visible subway graffiti, it is also the case that the city played a vital role in *developing* graffiti writing culture.

In Chap. 3, I explore this newly minted graffiti writing culture by drawing from field observations and in-depth interview material. While a portion of contemporary graffiti is still produced in an illegal manner, and while many paint illegally and legally, it is also the case that many current graffiti writers, especially for the sake of painting more elaborate murals, work within the perimeters of legality. This suggests that graffiti writing culture must now be understood as a much more complex and multi-faceted culture. Such an approach and understanding of graffiti is not one that we can readily discern in earlier accounts. Moreover, it is clear that the transition to legal graffiti is accompanied by an embracing of conventional values and lifestyles, and a desire to find a place within society. This, of course, calls into question the proclivity to imagine graffiti as a zone of "resistance" or "hostility" directed against a dominant culture.

Chapter 4 explores how this new graffiti writing culture has been received by the broader society within which it finds itself embedded. Drawing once again from ethnographic fieldwork, I show that much of the general public—and this despite all the claims of the political elite to the contrary—not only embraces, but also appreciates some types of graffiti, especially the legal and more colorful murals. This chapter also reveals how graffiti has managed to carve out a relatively stable space for itself within New York City's art world and within consumer society. In this connection, we will see further evidence to support the view that graffiti writers actually seek to be recognized by their broader social environment. In short, Chap. 4 is ultimately a story about the growing public tolerance, if not acceptance, of graffiti writing as a part of the urban environment.

Having outlined the contours of a new graffiti writing culture and some aspects of its position within society, Chap. 5 turns to an exploration of how city officials have reacted to the stubborn perseverance of public writing. Here we discover a political elite that is profoundly out of touch with, if not in a state of denial over, a new historical reality that they—paradoxically enough to be sure—helped to create. Based on an analysis of hundreds of newspaper articles and press releases from political administrations, Chap. 5 will show that a very Orwellian idea of truth governs the discourse of political elites. This notion will be explored more concretely through the sociological concept of moral panic. In this context, this will amount to showing that the kinds of claims that political elites make about graffiti, especially the suggestion that it entails disastrous social and economic consequences for those who reside within the city, are wildly overexaggerated. Indeed, it turns out to be the case that there is next to no support for the ways in which the political elite frame and make sense of graffiti writing culture.

But demonstrating that public officials operate with a very peculiar notion of truth when it comes to understanding graffiti, and that what we have on our hands is a case of moral panic, only provides us with *description*. What is left in abeyance is the problem of how to *explain* the city's official reaction to graffiti: If what we are encountering is a discourse that bears a tenuous connection to reality, then from where does it originate? What is being reflected in this discourse? It is to this problem that Chap. 6 turns. Whereas previous approaches to the problem of moral panics have understood them as motivated by the need to rearticulate foundational social norms, or the need to preserve capitalism, and sometimes as reflecting the desire to regulate the human body, I will argue that this particular panic is consistent with the punitive tendencies that inevitably accompany neoliberalism. Closely related, it also reflects an urban agenda in which public space is understood as a commodity. Perceiving the urban environment as a commodity entails, inter alia, the goal of creating spaces that resonate with the tastes and dispositions of wealthier social classes and, closely related, the protracted attempt to manipulate property values.

By reading the discourse produced by political elites against the grain, Chap. 6 will also show that the cozy relationship between the city leaders, broader neoliberal agendas, and the imperative toward urban "growth" is not an arrangement from which everybody stands to benefit. Rather, as social and urban space is increasingly adjusted to the dispositions and interests of privileged classes, those who occupy marginalized locations are likely to find themselves priced out of the city or, even worse, entangled within the carceral complex.

CHAPTER 2

# The Extraction of Subway Graffiti: The Late 1960s to 1989

**Abstract** Drawing on previous scholarship, this chapter provides a brief history of graffiti writing as it developed in New York City throughout the 1970s and the 1980s. It maps the prolonged "war against graffiti" that was orchestrated by public officials and the mass print media, and eventually ensured the demise of subway graffiti. However, the chapter concludes by suggesting that state opposition to graffiti, combined with appreciation from the art world and cultural industries, merely forced the art form "above ground," compelling it to find new avenues of expression.

**Keywords** Subway graffiti · Art worlds · Popular culture · Broken windows · Political elites

The year 1989 marked a radical turning point in the history of New York City's graffiti writing culture. It would be impossible, however, to understand the post-1989 "clean train" era without providing a historical overview of the 1970s and the 1980s. Four main actors will occupy our historical stage. First, and most obviously, the graffiti writers who developed an aesthetic sensibility that provided the basis for a new subcultural group. Second, the political elites and mass media who, joining forces in a moral crusade, waged a 20-year "war" against graffiti. At great expense, this "war" was fought along discursive and practical lines. Third, segments

© The Author(s) 2017
R. Kramer, *The Rise of Legal Graffiti Writing in New York and Beyond*, DOI 10.1007/978-981-10-2800-7_2

of the art world that sought to commodify graffiti and by doing so invested it with a sense of monetary and cultural value. Finally, the culture industry that, in a range of books, films, and documentaries, portrayed graffiti as "hip." The art world and cultural media not only interpreted graffiti in ways that radically differed from the state and mass media, but also facilitated the establishment of a global graffiti writing community.

Taking advantage of hindsight and previous scholarship, this chapter suggests that the 1970–1989 period can best be understood as one in which history was unfolding "behind the backs" of its actors. Its themes are linked by a subterranean thread: growing and developing in the subway system, graffiti was also being exiled from this domain and, somewhat ironically, pushed "above ground." To put it metaphorically, it is almost as if graffiti writing culture, eagerly observed by a handful of very different social institutions, each struggling over its meaning, was a seed buried in the earth's surface. While the city anticipated nothing of graffiti but pernicious weeds and acted accordingly, cultural institutions tended to see something that could be cultivated and included in the urban landscape. However, very few could foresee the new graffiti writing culture that eventually came to grow out of this concatenation of forces.

## The Emergence of Graffiti as a Creative Practice: "Tags," "Pieces," and "Throw-ups"

Toward the end of the 1960s in Philadelphia, the name "Cornbread" was particularly visible on modes of public transportation and along public transport routes.[1] The appearance of the name did not differ much from other forms of graffiti in public view at the time, yet its prevalence throughout the city suggested that this writing had little to do with "gang culture" or the need to signify the borders of "gang turf." Having achieved a degree of notoriety for his name writing habits, "Cornbread" was once interviewed by Jack Stewart in which he said, "I just started with a magic marker and worked up."[2] An idea that is central to graffiti writing culture is embedded in this seemingly straightforward statement: graffiti is a *project*, one in which individuals work toward subcultural recognition by "getting up."

---

[1] Powers, *Art of Getting Over* (1999).
[2] CORNBREAD quoted in Stewart, "Subway Graffiti," 157 (1989).

## 2 THE EXTRACTION OF SUBWAY GRAFFITI: THE LATE 1960S TO 1989    11

The contagious nature of graffiti was evident by the late 1960s and the early 1970s. The routes of busses and subway trains, as well as the buses and trains in Philadelphia, were adorned by many names. Perhaps because of its minimalist nature, writing one's name in public could be perceived as a culture in which participation was open to all. All you needed was a name, a marker, and the determination to write in public. This "open" aspect remains a key ingredient of writing culture. The results, however, have been and continue to be mixed. On the one hand, writing culture seems to spread and retain a large number of participants. On the other, the fact that one can receive recognition on the basis of quantity alone has assured that the quality of writing remains uneven. To be sure, any given creative endeavor tends to invite a large number of participants and generate a wide variety of forms, some of which possess more or less aesthetic merit than others. The difference with writing culture, and this perhaps helps to explain the negative way in which it is sometimes perceived, is that it is an inherently public culture. Whereas other creative endeavors, such as music or fine art, are filtered through the music industry, radio stations, galleries, and so on, graffiti remains unregulated, its aesthetic accomplishments and failures exposed.[3]

Graffiti had spread to New York City by 1971. Well-known writers of the time included "Junior 161," "Julio 204," and "Taki 183." Of the three, "Taki" was the most prolific and therefore recognizable name. As a messenger dependent on public transportation, he had the opportunity to write on trains and throughout the city.[4] That his name traveled via trains assisted the development of writing cultures already in the process of forming within various parts of New York City, such as the Bronx. But writing culture was also spreading south and east of Manhattan.

Public writing quickly became so extensive that the *New York Times* asked a reporter to track down "Taki 183" and produce a story about the new phenomenon. Entitled "'TAKI 183' spawns pen pals," the article has become a part of graffiti's folklore and it is often claimed that it drastically changed writing culture.[5] Apparently, by associating some meaning with

---

[3] For filtering of other cultural forms, see for example Becker, *Art worlds* (1982); Gitlin, "Movies" (1991); Hirsch, "Fads and Fashions" (1972).

[4] See Cooper and Chalfant, *Subway Art* (1984).

[5] "'TAKI 183,'" 37; Cooper and Chalfant, *Subway Art*, 14; Austin, *Taking the Train*, 49; Stewart, "Subway Graffiti," 232.

the practice—no matter how accurate or inaccurate this may have been—the article invited more people to partake in graffiti writing. The article is also credited with engendering a certain consciousness among many graffiti writers. Although not quite "fame" in the usual sense, writers learned that they might achieve notoriety not only among other like-minded individuals, but the general public as well.

With the growth in interest among New York City youth, several new developments occurred. As the insides of trains became covered with names, many writers searched for distinctive styles that would set themselves apart from the rest. Many of them also started writing on the exterior surfaces of subway cars, which were relatively free of graffiti. By the summer months of 1970, many writers discovered that they could enter the lay-ups and yards where trains were parked at night and during off-peak hours.[6] Here they found access to many cars, but they also learned that they had more time to produce their work. Over the next 3 years, from 1971 to 1973, the foundations necessary to set an aesthetic movement in motion were established.

The most effective way to portray the developments of these years is through reference to the three major forms associated with writing culture: "tags," "throw-ups," and "pieces." To think of "tags" as signatures would be slightly anachronistic in relation to the early 1970s. At this stage, tags more closely resembled a writer's general handwriting style. The extent to which early tags were stylized varied from writer to writer. Only a small percentage of these early tags displayed a strong sense of expressive concern. The idea of stylizing a tag such that it could be called a signature or "hand-style" was a later development (Fig. 2.1).

It was from this first form that the "piece" was developed. As Stewart shows, an early form of the piece appeared on the sides of New York City subway cars as early as 1971 by "Evil Ed" and "Cliff 159."[7] These pieces would best be described as relatively large-scale tags that were painted with one color and then outlined with a different color. This produced pieces with letters that had some breadth brought into relief by the use of a second outline color. The limitations imposed by this procedure for creating masterpieces were quickly discovered. In drawing the letters

---

[6] Cooper and Chalfant, *Subway Art*, 34; Stewart, "Subway Graffiti," 239; Castleman, *Getting Up* (1982).

[7] Stewart, "Subway Graffiti," 261–273.

## 2 THE EXTRACTION OF SUBWAY GRAFFITI: THE LATE 1960S TO 1989

**Fig. 2.1** An example of an early tag by "Cornbread." Photo by Ramon Been3 Vasquez

first, with the intention of preserving them as part of the finished piece, the expressive impact achieved by a writer was restricted to the basic form they initially produced. However, writers were quick to improve the procedure by plotting out letters first, filling them in, and then going back to reoutline them. This produced letters with greater impact due to their increased clarity.

Once the basic procedure for producing a "piece" was known, the range of aesthetic possibilities within graffiti exploded. Letters got bigger and bolder, eventually covering the entire side of a subway car. Alongside experimentation with size, new ways of stylizing letters quickly emerged. In 1972, "Top Cat 126" created what Stewart identifies as the first cohesive piece in terms of letter style. The typeface he produced came to be known as "Broadway Elegant."[8] Around this time, "Phase 2" developed a letter style that came to be known as the "softie" or "softie letters." As the name implies, these letters were defined by soft, round edges. But by cutting off round edges, overlapping, and connecting letters, "Phase 2" produced a style that looked complicated and "mechanical." "Tracy 168" specialized in this form of lettering but called them "wildstyle" letters—a term that was subsequently adopted by many of writing culture's practitioners. Despite variation in lettering styles, most forms came to be understood according to a continuum ranging from "wildstyle" to "straight letter." In other words, letter forms were primarily thought in terms of their legibility (Figs. 2.2 and 2.3).[9]

**Fig. 2.2** An example of a "straight letter" piece by "Wane," which incorporates the "cast shadow" effect. Photo by Luna Park

---

[8] Ibid., 292.
[9] Cooper and Chalfant, *Subway Art*, 70–71.

**Fig. 2.3** An example of a "wildstyle" piece by "Logek." Note the "flat 3D" effect. Photo by Roman Akkerman

Alongside the proliferation of letter styles, developments were occurring in relation to the ways in which any given letter could achieve expressive impact. More recent methods for constructing a piece allowed writers to add details and design elements—such as carefully drawn drips, bubbles/dots, stars, geometric shapes—to the insides of their letters (Fig. 2.4).

Three kinds of depth effect were also incorporated into the emerging styles. There was the "flat 3D" effect, which made a piece appear as though it were a colored, illustrative representation of a physical object. "Pistol" and "Flint 707," taking a different approach, rendered their letters as if rendering physical objects. This made the letters seem as though one was encountering actual physical objects, as opposed to their representation. The third depth effect involved conceptualizing letters as though they had been cut from a solid sheet, raised a little from the train's surface, and casting a shadow as a result. Of the three depth-effects, the "flat 3D" and the cast shadow would become the most common and widespread among writers. Although this trend continues to the present day, the "real 3D" letterform pioneered by "Pistol" and "Flint 707" is becoming more popular (Fig. 2.5).

The other key aesthetic element that emerged around this time was the "cloud." By 1973, the number of people actively writing graffiti had grown to such proportions that it was hard to find space on the trains. The cloud cleared up the background of a piece so that viewers would be less distracted by the tags of other writers and prevented disputes between

**Fig. 2.4** Four types of design features within letters. Photos by Ronald Kramer

writers. Since its inception, one of the accepted codes of writing culture was respect for the work of others. But with space filling fast, writers had little choice but to go over other people's names. Hence, the idea behind the cloud was that if you were going to cover somebody, you should cover them completely. The rule works on the premise that if an insult or offense cannot be seen, then it is as if no offense ever occurred. As writers realized that the cloud enhanced the impact of their names, it became something of an aesthetic element of the piece in its own right. The cloud soon

2 THE EXTRACTION OF SUBWAY GRAFFITI: THE LATE 1960S TO 1989    17

**Fig. 2.5** A piece by "Kezam" that embodies the "real 3D" letterform. Photo by Ronald Kramer. For examples of the "cast shadow" and "flat 3D" effect, see Figs. 2.2 and 2.3, respectively. See also Stewart, "Subway Graffiti" (1989); Cooper and Chalfant, *Subway Art* (1984); Schmidlapp and PHASE2, *Style Writing* (1996)

became known as "background" and served as a space in which a writer could create landscapes or scenery, or even tell some kind of visual story (Fig. 2.6).

Due to the many graffiti writers committed to piecing, an ability to execute "softie" letters soon became an expected dimension of a writer's repertoire. This general ability led to the creation of a third form of writing: the "throw-up." Usually sketched, filled in, and outlined very fast, throw-ups resemble simplified letters (Fig. 2.7).

Although varying from writer to writer, once a throw-up is developed it tends to remain more or less the same throughout an individual's writing career. In this regard, it is very similar to the development of one's tag. As a writer becomes intimately familiar with their tag and throw-up style—or styles—the amount of time a writer requires to execute these forms diminishes. The throw-up therefore occupies a strange place in writing

**Fig. 2.6** Painted by "Nme," a piece with cloud/background. Photo by Roman Akkerman. See also Cooper and Chalfant, *Subway Art* (1984)

**Fig. 2.7** A "throw-up" by "Baby 168." Photo by Ronald Kramer

culture: after growing out of the masterpiece, which was an outgrowth of the tag, the throw-up came to embody a dual history and now sits somewhere between them. As such, the throw-up inherited two early meanings within writing culture: on the one hand, it represents a succinct statement of a writer's style and therefore gives some indication of one's personal history within writing culture. On the other, to the extent that the creative energy behind its development mirrors that of the tag, it can also be used for the purpose of coverage or "getting up." In this sense, it combines elements of the tag and the piece. Painting a lot of throw-ups is sometimes considered the equivalent of painting a lot of minor or basic pieces. As "Cap," a notorious train writer from the late 1970s and the early 1980s, once put it: "The object is more. Not the biggest or the beautiful-est. A *little piece* on every car is what counts. Not one whole car on every 10 cars that goes by."[10]

Since becoming an established practice, the throw-up has remained controversial within writing culture and its broader sociocultural and spatial context. Some writers feel that throw-ups lack any aesthetic merit and subtract from writing culture as a whole.[11] The public tends to find them ugly and they are without doubt the most despised form of public writing. Yet, their importance to writing culture is hard to deny.[12]

OFFICIAL REACTIONS I: THE TROPE OF "WAR," TECHNOLOGY, AND THE ERADICATION OF GRAFFITI WRITING

From the late 1960s to 1972, as *writing* was becoming its own *cultural world*, a form of collective consciousness that transcended its individual members, the mass media generally thought the phenomenon unnewsworthy. Stewart, for example, found one instance in which the term "graffiti" appeared in the *New York Times* in 1967. On this occasion, the newspaper was referring to a new poster produced by the Metropolitan Transport Authority (MTA) that advised passengers on proper subway

---

[10] CAP quoted in Silver and Chalfant, *Style Wars* (1983), emphasis added.
[11] See Cooper and Chalfant, *Subway Art*, 74; BUTCH 2 quoted in Miller, *Aerosol Kingdom*, 123; Lachmann, "Graffiti as Career," 241; DOC TC5 quoted in Austin, *Taking the Train*, 244.
[12] Austin, *Taking the Train*, 115.

conduct. That graffiti appeared on a list of "don'ts" along with things like "don't fare evade" indicates the extent to which the MTA found it a problem.[13] Prior to 1972, there were no laws in New York City specifically related to public writing and those caught were usually turned over to parents who, it was assumed, would discipline their children.[14]

Things were about to change. The volume of subway graffiti in the early 1970s led the *New York Times* to construe it as a "problem." Initially perceived as a quirky behavior, the graffiti kids were apparently getting carried away. Quite suddenly, graffiti was framed as an "epidemic" and its producers cast as a "menace" to society. In the wake of such representations, the City Council deemed a "war on graffiti" necessary, a rhetorical trope that went on to become a perennial feature of news reporting on writing.[15]

Following the perspective advocated by the print media and the City Council, Mayor John Lindsay and the MTA developed an interest in eradicating writing culture. In the summer of 1972, Lindsay began drafting what would become the first antigraffiti law within New York City. The bill, signed into law a few months later, made it unlawful to carry a can of spray paint in any public facility.[16] The significance of this approach lies in the fact that it set in motion a repressive stance to writing culture among city officials that no mayor has since challenged.

The other major strategy of Lindsay's administration involved putting pressure on the MTA to take greater responsibility for combating graffiti. Lindsay repeatedly asked the MTA to increase surveillance and security in lay-ups and yards. For him, security ultimately meant installing fences to prevent writers from accessing train storage yards. Although the MTA more or less ignored these suggestions, they were increasing their efforts. The MTA focused on policing, making arrests, pursuing what they saw as appropriate sentences, and the removal of writing. If one is measuring according to the extent to which they corroded writing culture, none of

---

[13] The article (Bernard Weinraub, "39 'Don'ts' Listed in Subways' Code," *New York Times*, February 17, 1967) is cited by Stewart, "Subway Graffiti," 160.
[14] Stewart, "Subway Graffiti," 267.
[15] See Austin's discussion, *Taking the Train*, 78–84.
[16] Stewart, "Subway Graffiti," 268–269.

## 2 THE EXTRACTION OF SUBWAY GRAFFITI: THE LATE 1960S TO 1989

these efforts could meaningfully be portrayed as successful. In fact, the initial efforts of the MTA were often counterproductive.

The MTA implemented what was perhaps their first coordinated attempt to conceal subway writing toward the end of 1973. At a cost of approximately $1,800 per car, and with 6,800 cars in the system, they decided to rapidly repaint the entire subway fleet.[17] However, those on the receiving end interpreted what the MTA imagined as a decisive blow to writing culture quite differently. For many writers, repainted surfaces are simply fresh canvases on which to produce new work.[18] To be sure, others interpreted the MTA's repainting as an insult that demanded retaliation. Thus, the repainting of 1973 did have an impact on writing culture, but not in the way intended or hoped for by the MTA. Some trains stayed free of writing for about a week. But as the MTA did not prevent writers from gaining access to storage yards and lay-ups—and this much to the ire of Lindsay and his antigraffiti project—the historical event of repainting the trains was quickly rendered invisible by layers of spray paint emanating from the energy, determination, and persistence of writers.

In 1977, the MTA found funding for two further antigraffiti enforcement efforts.[19] The first of these involved establishing an antigraffiti Vandal Squad, which had grown to 22 members by 1980. Those less committed to graffiti may have been discouraged by the presence of the police, but among the more committed this simply raised the stakes of the game: as police began to raid yards and lay-ups to catch writers, the daring required to successfully execute large works became highly respected. For many, then, an increased police presence was incorporated into the prestige economy of writers and amounted to further encouragement.[20]

The second, and more significant of the MTA's antigraffiti enforcement efforts, was the introduction of what writers refer to as "the buff." At a cost of approximately $20 million, "the buff" is basically a large, glorified car wash in which trains are driven through a shower of powerful paint removing chemicals and then rinsed off.[21] The desirability of the aesthetic

---

[17] Ibid., 386.
[18] See Chap. 4. See also Halsey and Young, "Our Desires" (2006).
[19] Austin, *Taking the Train*, 128.
[20] Cooper and Chalfant, *Subway Art*, 99.
[21] Austin, *Taking the Train*, 130–132; See also Silver and Chalfant, *Style Wars* (1983).

result is debatable: the chemical solvent was often more successful at removing the base coat of paint originally applied to the train car. Alternatively, the base coat of paint and the paint applied by writers tended to melt into a hideous color that looked as if it had been haphazardly smeared over the train's exterior.[22] Even Richard Ravitch, the then chairman of the MTA, conceded that after having been "cleaned" in this manner, trains were far from pleasant to look at: "Often what you get is a vomitous looking car which some of the graffiti artists describe as less attractive than their art."[23] Nevertheless, if measured according to proficiency of destroying masterpieces, "the buff" represented a significant advance over earlier efforts.

These strategies were not inconsequential to the development of writing culture. Those committed to piecing were dismayed to see works destroyed with greater frequency. But the buff did ensure a steady supply of "fresh canvas" that encouraged aesthetic exploration. As writers learned that a piece may not go into circulation at all, or may only run in the subway system for a very short time, they responded with an increased reliance on photography to preserve their works—a technology that would go on to become central to the survival of writing culture. On the other hand, a greater police presence and the buff also tipped the balance in favor of bombing with throw-ups. Many writers reasoned that if the MTA was simply going to destroy graffiti, it was pointless to waste one's time and paint producing detailed work.[24] Despite such circumstances, writing culture was thriving to such an extent that its demise seemed unimaginable. This is evident in a remark once made by "Dez," a very prominent writer of the time: "Rather than try to make your first piece be a burner and it looks wak, just work your way up. *The trains ain't goin' nowhere.*"[25] As the 1970s drew to a close, the continued belief in the possibility of erasing writing culture from the subway system probably appeared to many as wishful thinking, perhaps even an absurd fantasy of sorts. Yet, by 1980, a second "war" on the new writing would be waged.

---

[22] Austin, *Taking the Train*, 131.
[23] Richard Ravitch quoted in Silver and Chalfant, *Style Wars* (1983).
[24] Austin, *Taking the Train*, 131.
[25] DEZ quoted in Cooper and Chalfant, *Subway Art*, 32, emphasis added.

## Official Reactions II: New Discursive Strategies and "War" by Other Means

In 1978, Edward Koch was elected mayor of New York City. His election coincided with a period in which many larger US cities were experiencing fiscal crises. This was largely the result of structural transformations occurring within the global economy and economic policies established at various levels of state. By 1980, New York City was gripped by a series of economically related problems. As the city moved toward bankruptcy, extreme poverty set in, youth unemployment rates were high, crime rates increased, and funding for essential city services was severely reduced.[26]

As is well known, one of the many casualties of this economic crisis was the subway system. Austin has noted how bad subway conditions were during the early 1980s. It is worth quoting him at length:

> A 1983 state inspection of the system reported that there were 300 "red tag zones" where track conditions were so poor that conductors were required to reduce train speeds by roughly 50 percent, to ten mph or less. Even if a train arrived on time, riders were frequently prevented from entering or leaving because the automatic sliding doors would fail to open...The system suffered 1800 car fires during 1981, 217 of which were listed as "major"...[B]etween 1977 and 1981, 69 subway train collisions and derailments occurred, 21 during 1981 alone. The number of train derailments increased to average of one every 18 days in 1983.[27]

Given the nature of these problems, the fact that a renewed "war on graffiti" emerged around 1980 is somewhat peculiar. After all, the writing on the trains did not produce any structural damage such that it could be said to affect their performance. There is, for example, obviously no connection between the presence of graffiti on a train and its derailment. Moreover, any material efforts to remove the writing were going to cost money that arguably could have been better spent. However, a new discursive formation buttressed the idea that a continuation of the "war" against graffiti was a worthwhile priority.

---

[26] Austin, *Taking the Train*, 143–144.
[27] Ibid., 135, 136. See also Daley, "City Subways on the Mend," B1 (1985).

As the 1970s came to a close, the mass media began to focus on the appearance of the urban environment. The significance of appearance was initially articulated in relation to the psychological state of city residents. It was held that visible interventions in public space that were not officially permitted by the state (such as writing) generated psychological malaise, depression, and cynicism in viewers or in those for whom such surroundings constituted their urban environment.[28]

Not content with establishing specious links between the appearance of the urban environment and the psychology of individuals, the media also "theorized" the broader social, political, and economic implications of "unauthorized" visual orders. It was suggested that graffiti was responsible for more severe forms of social disorder, such as rampant general lawlessness and serious crime. Politically, unauthorized visual interventions came to be associated with the belief that "nobody cares and things are out of control." Economically, graffiti was posited as a cause of "urban decline" for a variety of reasons, such as its ability to convince corporations to leave the city, produce "slums," depreciate real estate values, and so on.[29]

Although several academics were quick to consecrate such ideas by rearticulating them with a (pseudo)scientific gloss, it was George L. Kelling and James Q. Wilson who came up with the buzzword that would neatly summarize these conservative beliefs about visual order and go on to inform much public policy on such matters: "broken windows." What Kelling and Wilson added was an emphasis on how to prevent the collapse of civic order that practices like painting graffiti supposedly entailed. If the problem was that minor signs of disorder invited serious

---

[28] Austin, *Taking the Train*, 144.

[29] For the supposed social, political, and economic significance of graffiti see Herman, "Vandals Take Psychological Toll," A1 (1971); Levine, "Transit Authority Proclaims," B1 (1986); Editorial, "Gaining on Graffiti," A26 (1986); Butterfield, "New York Walls," B1; Pollack, "Islip Moving," 20 (1985); Bass, "For Graffiti Artists," Section 11CN, 2 (1986); Whitney, "New Plague," A9 (1988). The idea that graffiti is responsible for the economic decline of cities and/or regions is preposterous given the sociological literature on the subject. Such accounts stress the importance of deindustrialization, taxing policies, competition between cities, banking practices, and state policies in explaining the economic (in)stability of cities. See, for example, Logan and Molotch, *Urban Fortunes* (1987).

acts of crime, the solution was to revoke the invite. This could be done by enforcing stricter laws and penalties upon those found responsible for the commission of minor misdeeds, which presupposed a greater police presence and increased surveillance.[30]

By the early 1980s, then, there existed a new discourse that accorded major importance to the visual appearance of the city. Despite its lack of empirical support,[31] it was not long before the MTA began complying with the practical logic embedded within the broken windows thesis. In the summer of 1980, they reinvigorated their efforts to repaint the subway fleet. Once again, however, this displeased the city's mayor. The problem, according to Koch, was obviously not that they were trying to conceal public writing, but that they did nothing to prevent writers from accessing the storage facilities in which trains were kept when not in service and in which writers went about doing their work.

Koch began using his access to the mass media to publicly shame the MTA for this oversight. Taking a page out of Lindsay's book, he suggested that the MTA construct security fences around the train yards and invest in some guard dogs. The MTA rejected this idea on the basis that the guard dogs might step on the third rail or attack young people. However, as Castleman's account suggests, they were more likely worried about the possibility of the guard dogs escaping and harming city residents as writers would cut holes in fences to enter storage yards.[32] In response, the mayor suggested that the MTA could construct two concentric fences and have a wolf run between the fences. This would prevent the wolf from stepping on the third rail. Koch also suggested that wolves would not attack humans unless first attacked.[33]

Within a year, the MTA had complied with the mayor's wishes and installed a trial fencing system around one of its storage yards. Topped with razor wire, concentric fences were built and guard dogs were placed between them. The strategy was relatively successful and the MTA decided—despite coming at a

---

[30] Wilson and Kelling, "Broken Windows," 29–38 (1982).
[31] See Wilson quoted in Hurley, "Scientists at Work," F1 (2004). See also Cohen, "Pie Chart is Half-Baked," B7 (2000).
[32] Castleman, *Getting Up*, 146 (1982); Goodman, "Dogs To Patrol," A1 (1981a).
[33] See Koch interviewed in Silver and Chalfant, *Style Wars* (1983).

cost of $22.4 million[34]—to secure the rest of its storage facilities in a similar way. If not displeased, the whole affair generated a smug response from Koch: it wasn't the cost that annoyed him, but the fact that the plan was "so successful and they [the MTA] now claim it as their own idea."[35]

The second initiative implemented by the MTA was the "clean car" program. During the early 1980s, when measured according to any service indicator, the MTA's performance had hit an extreme low point. This generated studies and public reporting on the MTA's management structure. As a way to keep public criticism at bay, TA president David Gunn and MTA chairman Robert Kiley decided to focus on the "cleanliness" of the subway system. Although they were concerned with dirt, litter, the stench of urine, and other comparable problems, "cleaning" the subway was quickly conflated with the absence of graffiti.[36] They announced as one of their relatively short-term goals the creation of a graffiti-free subway system.[37]

In striving to fulfill this goal, Gunn and Kiley relied on a variety of strategies. By far the most extraordinary measure was their decision to withhold fully functional trains from service to prevent graffiti from circulating in public view. This policy applied at all times, which meant that morning schedules were altered and less trains were moving through the system even during rush hours.[38] If during the 1970s the MTA were prepared to sacrifice the aesthetic appearance of the subway because of visible public writing, by the 1980s it would seem they were prepared to

[34] Austin, *Taking the Train*, 209.
[35] The Koch quote is from Silver and Chalfant, *Style Wars* (1983). For the other points and information supplied see Smothers, "Koch Calls For," B3 (1980); Goodman, "Pits of Barbed Wire," B1 (1981b); Haitch, "Thwarting Graffiti," Section 1, 42 (1982).
[36] Levine, "Transit Authority Proclaims," B1 (1986); Douglas, Connelly and Mansnerus, "Wondering Where," Section 4, 7 (1986). Of course, "cleaning" in this context should be taken in the anthropological sense of correcting "matter out of place." See Douglas, *Purity and Danger* (1984).
[37] The safety and reliability of the subway did not begin to improve until 1987/1988. However, by this time the subway was generally "cleaner." See Douglas and Connelly, "Riding Cleaner," Section 4, 7 (1986).
[38] Austin, *Taking the Train*, 219 (2001); Hays, "Transit Agency," A1; Butterfield, "New York Walls," B1.

sacrifice efficient and dependable transportation. This gives some indication of how powerful a symbol public writing had become.

Initially the approach of Gunn and Kiley had only limited success. But by the mid-1980s, as writers began to learn that the chances of their work circulating throughout the system were slim to none, the TA came close to achieving their stated goal of maintaining a "graffiti-free" subway.[39] Finally, on May 12, 1989, after a long 20-year battle involving massive financial expenditures, the New York City subway was declared to be "graffiti free."[40] Almost needless to say, within the mass media and among city leaders, the accomplishment was highly celebrated. To such actors, the absence of public writing on the subway system was a sure sign that the proper authorities had "saved" a city that came close to collapse.[41]

But this claim was rather misleading. The idea that the financial recovery of the city was the result of a change in the appearance of the subway obviously ignores the years of material hardship and sacrifice forced upon many of the city's residents. Furthermore, the claim that the subway was "graffiti free" constituted a grossly inaccurate representation of the aesthetic order of things. The subway system was not, and is still not, graffiti free. Tunnels are covered in graffiti; trains still get painted (although the public rarely gets to see those trains in circulation) and new forms, such as "scratchiti" and "etch" bombing, were discovered to mark the windows of subway cars (Fig. 2.8).

Much more obviously, a very large portion of the public writing that the authorities did manage to keep off the subway system simply resurfaced in other public spaces. Writing was not eradicated from the underground subway. It would be much more accurate to say that throughout

---

[39] Mincer, "War On Grime?" 24 (1985).
[40] Schmidlapp and Phase 2, *Style Writing*, 112; Bennet, "New Arsenal," Section 4, 2 (1992).
[41] Editorial, "Man Who Saved," A16 (1990a); Editorial, "New York Transit," A22 (1990b); Strom, "Transit Official Outlines," 21 (1991); Miles, "In the Subway," Section 4, 24. Yet this latter article also reveals that despite the absence of graffiti, the number of robberies and assaults in the subway increased. A point later acknowledged in Kelling and Bratton, "Declining Crime Rates" (1998), who are proponents of the theory.

**Fig. 2.8** "Scratchiti" and "etch" bombing. Photos by Ronald Kramer

the 1970s and the 1980s the city was effectively squeezing graffiti out of the subway system and pushing it above ground.[42]

How writing culture eluded the expensive "wars" waged against it by political elites is a complicated story. While its survival has much to do with the passion and desires of graffiti writers, segments of the art world and

---

[42] Farrelly, "Light of Day," Section 1, 26 (1989); Licata, "Midnight Writers," Section 12LI, 32 (1989); Berger, "Uphill Battle," 27 (1990).

other forms of cultural media also played an important role. Such "cultural industries" are more likely to see graffiti as a commodity from which profit can be derived. Although problematic in some respects, the tendency to exploit graffiti often entails investing it with new meanings that are likely to challenge the definitions offered by the state.

## ART WORLDS AND CULTURAL MEDIA

In 1972, Hugo Martinez formed United Graffiti Artists (UGA) while a sociology student at New York University. Although not an active graffiti writer, Martinez believed that the people painting subway cars were producing a form of art, but that this energy needed to be transferred to canvas to receive the social recognition that it deserved. There were several criteria for joining the group. Most notably in this context, membership was highly selective and demanded that a writer stop painting trains, which some did, but not all of them. On December 7, 1972, having acquired space from the City College, Martinez curated and opened the first "graffiti art" show. It was called the "City College Writer's Exhibition." After this show, the UGA continued to pursue their creativity in socially acceptable arenas. In April of 1973, they painted backdrops while Twyla Tharps's "Deuce Coupe" was being performed on stage. A few months later, they opened another show at the Razor Gallery in New York City. Soon after this, they were shown at the Chicago Museum of Science and Technology.[43]

In response to the "elitism" of Martinez's UGA, Jack Pelsinger formed Nation of Graffiti Artists (NOGA) in 1974, which, unlike its predecessor, was open to all. Pelsinger encouraged writers to expand their horizons in various directions. While he did see the viability of transferring graffiti onto canvas, he also saw commercial potential in privately commissioned murals, advertising, and other similar outlets. In September of 1975, UGA and non-UGA members put on another group show at the Artists Space Gallery in SoHo.[44]

The relationship between graffiti and art worlds seemed to dissolve for the remainder of the 1970s. However, it was soon rekindled in 1979 when

---

[43] Castleman, *Getting Up*, 117–126.
[44] Ibid., 126–133.

Claudio Bruni, after seeing LEE's elaborate graffiti murals in New York City, decided to exhibit some of his paintings at Galleria Medusa in Rome. Throughout 1980 and 1981, "graffiti" was incorporated in a variety of shows and exhibits: Henry Chalfant's photographic documentation of graffiti was displayed at the OK Harris gallery; the Colab Arts Group featured the work of several writers in their month-long show at Times Square; Diego Rivera put on the "New York/New Wave" show at PS1; and Haring curated a downtown "graffiti art" show at the Mudd Club. Alternative art spaces, such as Fashion Moda in the Bronx, the Fun Gallery, 51X, and Graffiti Above Ground, also emerged and often exhibited the work of those associated with writing culture.[45]

Many of these shows were attended by critics who often ended up writing articles for the mainstream press and highly respected publications within the art world.[46] Although reactions were mixed, representatives of the art world did forge a discourse in which signifiers such as "graffiti writer" and "artist" circulated in the same orbit. As controversial as it may have been to some, there was now a cultural and material context beyond writing culture that enabled writers to interpret graffiti as a legitimate, creative pursuit.

Alongside the art world, other media were absorbing graffiti writing culture as well. Although not unknown to the 1970s, it was the 1980s that witnessed the production of some highly successful films, documentaries, and books on graffiti. Given the mass audience it is likely to attract, such media were arguably of more significance than the art world in terms of exposing graffiti to the world. Moreover, the cultural media in question are less likely to demand that practitioners of writing culture change the nature of their production. For example, a documentary does not require the artists to produce works on canvas for inclusion. Thus, unlike the art world, cultural media tends to document and record already existing modes of expression. As such, it is much more capable of producing a visual text that comes closer to approximating cultural forms in their original contexts.

---

[45] Austin, *Taking the Train*, 190–191.
[46] See Austin, *Taking the Train*, 186–192; Hager, *Hip Hop*, 59–79; Miller, *Aerosol Kingdom*, 158–160; Schwartzman, *Street Art* (1985).

## 2 THE EXTRACTION OF SUBWAY GRAFFITI: THE LATE 1960S TO 1989    31

Among the major movies released in the 1980s were *Wild Style* (1982)[47] and *Beat Street* (1984).[48] In terms of documentaries, *Style Wars*[49] was released in 1983. A variety of articles and books, some more academically oriented than others, were published throughout the 1970s and the 1980s. In 1974, *The Faith of Graffiti* was released.[50] This was a coffee table book consisting of photos taken by Mervyn Kurlansky and Jon Naar, and a written text by Norman Mailer. Mailer's text was noteworthy for interpreting writing culture through rhetorical conventions associated with Art History. In 1982, Castleman's *Getting Up* was released; Hager's *Hip-Hop* and Cooper and Chalfant's *Subway Art* were released in 1984; Schwartzman's *Street Art* came out in 1985; and Cooper and Prigoff published *Spraycan Art* in 1987.

It is well beyond the scope of this chapter to provide a detailed analysis of the ways in which graffiti writing was represented in each of these texts. What is important to note here is the role that they played in ensuring the survival of graffiti writing culture. Most important in this connection were Cooper and Chalfant's *Subway Art*, the films *Wild Style* and *Beat Street*, and the documentary *Style Wars*. By far the most significant book in terms of exposing graffiti to national and international audiences, *Subway Art* could easily be described as the glossy print version of *Style Wars*. It featured 239 color photographs. Most of these were of paintings done on New York City subway trains, but some showed writers at work in the yards or during other stages involved in the painting process. The photos did a remarkable job of conveying the excitement and energy of both the process of painting and the finished products. *Subway Art* also situated these practices and works within their sociocultural contexts by including snippets of information concerning writing culture's history, its norms, values, and vocabulary, the social relations among writers, and the political opposition with which it was met.

The films *Wild Style* and *Beat Street*, along with *Style Wars*, were not concerned exclusively with graffiti. Rather, they produced and disseminated a new body of knowledge concerning the cultural practices being

---

[47] Ahearn, *Wild Style* (1982).
[48] Belafonte and Picker, *Beat Street* (1984).
[49] Silver and Chalfant, *Style Wars* (1983).
[50] Mailer, *Faith of Graffiti* (1974).

developed by many of New York City's younger residents. Irrespective of the conscious intentions of the producers, it was these films that established commonsensical understandings of the term "hip-hop." They suggested that hip-hop was a culture of three "elements": graffiti, rapping, and break-dancing. To many writers, insofar as this definition tended to suggest the simultaneous emergence and congruence of hip-hop's "elements," it was historically and socioculturally inaccurate. Not only did writing culture precede rap and breaking by approximately a decade, but many practitioners of writing had nothing to do with rapping and breaking. The following remarks made by "Sonic," "Lady Pink," and "Part"— writers who began their graffiti careers prior to "hip-hip"—are suggestive:

> Now they characterize graffiti as being under hip-hop with the rapping and all that, which is not all true because you have writers like IZ THE WIZ, QUIK and SACH—a lot of different writers—these guys listened to rock. What happened to Rock and Roll? Rock and Roll should have been part of hip-hop also.[51]
>
> I think that "hip-hop," the term, was coined in the very early '80s, '81 maybe, or something like '82, and graffiti was thrown in there sort of like a background art. I don't really feel hip-hop. I'm not even sure what hip-hop is, but they call me hip-hop. I don't think so. Graffiti was around more than a decade before.[52]
>
> I never really embraced [hip-hop]...I never really embraced that intertwining because it's really different worlds that they're trying to make into one.[53]

However, beyond the distortions entailed by defining hip-hop, it is important to note that the term, insofar as it labeled a diversity of aesthetic practices, made it possible for commercial interests to transform subcultural activities into cultural commodities.[54] Whereas the extent to which rapping and DJ-ing were commodified is well known and now obvious,[55]

---

[51] Author's interview with SONIC.
[52] Author's interview with LADY PINK.
[53] Author's interview with PART TDS.
[54] Miller, *Aerosol Kingdom*, 162–167.
[55] Rose, *Black Noise* (1994); Chang, *Can't Stop, Won't Stop* (2005); George, *Hip Hop America* (1998).

the commercial history of breaking and graffiti has received less attention. Although a history of breaking is beyond the scope of the present work, it can be noted that it did manage to carve out a relatively small space for itself within mass culture. For example, it often appeared as part of rap performances, in rap music videos, and sometimes in commercials.

Like break-dancing, writing was also quick to find space for itself in relation to rap music. Most obviously, the aesthetics of graffiti often appeared on record covers, advertisements for rap shows, and so on. Yet, of hip-hop's three elements, graffiti was by far the hardest to commodify. It was one thing to use graffiti on a record cover to insinuate the "street cred" of the latest rap artist; another matter altogether to profit from writing culture in a manner comparable to the kind of revenue that could be generated from record sales. As such, writing culture struggled to find a stable space for itself within commercial spheres.

Despite being less susceptible to commercialization, graffiti writing culture was encouraged by films like *Style Wars* and books such as *Subway Art*. In suggesting that hip-hop was a culture, such texts invested graffiti, rapping, and breaking with new meanings. Referring to hip-hop as a "culture" is, in some respects, comparable to framing graffiti as "art." Both terms generally identify products that ought to be appreciated and, in this sense, have a normative undertow that accords whatever is so designated a kind of immunity from the moral and legal condemnation that seeks to push certain modes of expression beyond the pale of "civility." This is, of course, not to say that framing hip-hop as culture was successful. Labeling is more often than not a contested process. Nevertheless, the attempt was made.

Furthermore, the mobility of visual media promoted a global interest in writing and writing culture. For a variety of reasons, people all over the world could identify with graffiti as soon as they saw it. In fact, that writing cultures rapidly developed in many parts of the world was clear by 1987 when Chalfant and Prigoff released *Spraycan Art*. In this book, one could find well-executed pieces in most major US cities, places such as London, the major cities of European nations, and regions as far from New York as Australia and New Zealand.

As graffiti spread to many parts of the world, a global writing community began to emerge. This was particularly important in helping New York City's writing culture, and writing cultures in general, withstand severe political opposition. While New York City officials may have been making advancements in keeping graffiti out of the subway system, writers were beginning to sense a new age of communications on the horizon. The absorption of graffiti by the art world and culture industry showed writers that channels existed for the circulation of their work. Within this context, one did not necessarily need to paint subway trains to have their work reach the public. One could paint any surface, document it—or be lucky enough to have others document it—and have reason to suspect that cultural fields and new technologies of communication will ensure the work reaches local and global audiences.

## Toward a New Future

Insofar as the history of graffiti writing culture is concerned, the 1970s and the 1980s represent a time in which a new aesthetic practice, one that was quite adventurous in many respects, rapidly developed. Heavily dependent on the subway system for publicly circulating its works, graffiti writing expanded in qualitative and quantitative directions. As the quality of graffiti was improving, it was also growing in volume. Given its visual punch, graffiti inevitably collided with a variety of powerful social institutions: the city's political elites, the mass media, art worlds, and cultural media. While the city devoted its resources to the eradication of graffiti, art worlds and cultural media sought to generate economic profits through its commodification.

Getting caught up in this maelstrom of forces was not without consequence for writing culture. As graffiti writers continued to compete and channel their energy in various directions, the city was slowly regaining control over the aesthetic appearance of the subway system. And yet, it was simply not the case that graffiti was in the process of being buried. Rather, through the persistence and dedication of graffiti writers, sympathetic segments of the art world, books, and movies and documentaries, it was beginning to seep to the surface where it would spread to other parts of the world. Indeed, by the end of the 1980s, it was difficult to deny that writing culture was well on its way to becoming a phenomenon of global proportions and that New York City's graffiti writers had adapted to a new set of circumstances.

While political elites were busy declaring that they had won the "war on graffiti" in New York City, it was clear that this was merely a "battle," so to speak. By no means had the city rendered graffiti a thing of the past. It would be more accurate to say that they, along with several others, played their part in creating a different future.

CHAPTER 3

# The "Clean Train" Era: Creating a Space for the Legal Production of Graffiti

**Abstract** Drawing from ethnographic fieldwork, this chapter explores the ways in which graffiti writing culture reinvented itself in the 1990s and opening years of the twenty-first century. It argues that while new forms of illegal graffiti have emerged, this period is also marked by the rise of legal graffiti. This latter development remains overlooked in contemporary scholarship, which tends to romanticize graffiti and often construes it as a politics of resistance. Against such interpretations, this chapter shows how those committed to painting with permission are deeply concerned about the aesthetic quality of public space and are more likely to seek social and cultural inclusion on the basis of their creative practices.

**Keywords** Legal graffiti · Street art · Ethnography · Consumer culture · Art worlds · Media · Resistance

As the subway era entered its twilight, graffiti writers forged new practices to ensure the survival of their aesthetic tradition. This quest for survival took several major routes. Although governed by a new logic, graffiti writing culture retains a strong commitment to painting subway trains. Alongside the ongoing desire to paint trains, much contemporary graffiti is focused on "street bombing." This typically entails painting tags and throw-ups on buildings, store front gates, highway embankments, and anything else within reach. Against these dynamics, however, the 1990s and opening decades of the twenty-first century have witnessed the rise of legal graffiti, which allows practitioners to ply their craft in ways that do not violate the law. In fact, legal graffiti rapidly expanded in the post-1989 era and now provides a breeding ground for the production of works that, due to their powerful visual impact, are noticeably distinct and tend to gain public approval.

Due to the general inclination to focus on New York City subway graffiti of the 1970s and the 1980s, or on illegal graffiti writing cultures in other regions of the world, previous academic analyses have tended to overlook the phenomenon of legal graffiti. As such, a detailed account of this new approach to graffiti writing and its significance is long overdue. Whereas previous scholarship tends to present graffiti as an illegal practice that adopts an "oppositional" stance toward society, the emergence of legal graffiti suggests that such an image is incomplete. With the transition to legal modes of production, many graffiti writers have come to embrace conventional values and have sought social acceptance for their creative outpourings.

## GRAFFITI AS AN "ILLEGAL SUBCULTURE" AND "POLITICAL RESISTANCE"

Most accounts of graffiti tend to assume it is an inherently illegal practice.[1] This is not surprising given that it is often produced in direct violation of the law and accompanied by other criminal activities, such as illegally entering train yards. In numerous accounts, especially those with a tendency to romanticize the practice, attention often turns toward how graffiti is over criminalized. Such criminalization is usually governed by political and economic ends, and involves investing "graffiti" with negative meanings that effectively rationalize strict antigraffiti legislation.[2]

---

[1] Mailer, *Faith of Graffiti* (1974); Castleman, *Getting Up* (1982); Lachmann, "Graffiti as Career" (1988); Ferrell, *Crimes of Style* (1993); Austin, *Taking the Train* (2001); Stewart, "Ceci Tuera Cela," 161–180; Spitz, *Image and Insight* (1991).

[2] See especially Castleman, *Getting Up* (1982); Ferrell, *Crimes of Style* (1993); and Austin, *Taking the Train* (2001) on this point.

In other accounts, illegality functions as an essential element in identifying the meaning of graffiti. According to Nancy Macdonald,[3] the illegality of graffiti constitutes "the subculture's backbone." Macdonald's evocation of the human body is not merely metaphorical: for it is the illegality of graffiti writing that allows for the construction of a masculine identity or character. As she puts it:

> This subculture must be acknowledged for what it is...a site for "male" youth—an illegal confine where danger, opposition and the exclusion of women is used to nourish, amplify and salvage notions of masculinity.[4]

In a somewhat related account that focuses on the subjective benefits that graffiti affords its participants, Campos argues that writing is an attractive subculture because it allows individuals to feel "heroic."[5] For Janice Rahn,[6] illegality does not so much ensure a space in which masculine identity can be developed, but one in which autonomy from dominant social groups can be won. Insofar as this autonomy is achieved through illegality, it becomes an "ethic" among graffiti writers and needs to be actively preserved:

> The community's ethics concerning graffiti's illegal status ensures that it cannot be entirely co-opted. As it becomes popularized, writers seem to push their art back to the margins of a clearly distinguishable underground culture. Members are dedicated to their own code of ethics.[7]

The illegality of graffiti often paves the way for a fascination with how writers violate the law in other respects. In Castleman's well-known account from the early 1980s, theft was so common among writers that it could be said to constitute a "tradition."[8] Moreover, it seems that some graffiti writers went so far as to turn their skills at shoplifting into a business enterprise of sorts: "There is an active black market among the

---

[3] Macdonald, *Graffiti Subculture*, 126.
[4] Macdonald, *Graffiti Subculture*, 149.
[5] Campos, "Graffiti Writer as Superhero" (2012).
[6] Rahn, *Painting without Permission* (2002).
[7] Ibid., 162.
[8] Castleman, *Getting Up*, 46.

writers, and experienced rack-up artists...can turn a profit filling orders for other writers."[9] On occasion, this proclivity for theft even led to the commission of burglary:

> Another spectacular rack-up...was not the result of chance discovery... [T]hree writers carefully planned and executed a late-night robbery at a warehouse in the Bronx, getting away with more than 2000 cans of spray paint. Only Rustoleum and Red Devil paint, the brands most preferred by writers, were taken.[10]

In Austin's account, the theft that constitutes a "tradition" for Castleman becomes a "virtue" that establishes a writer's "street cred" and commitment to the subculture's "ethical code." Since "the quantity of paint needed for a piece was beyond the economic means of most writers, necessity was made a virtue, and theft or swapping were considered the only ethical means of acquiring paint."[11]

Alongside the focus on graffiti writing as a culture that operates on the "wrong side of legality," one also finds the notion that it adopts an oppositional stance toward the dominant society by which it is surrounded. Based on an analysis of graffiti throughout the late 1980s and the early 1990s in Denver, Colorado, Ferrell finds that "the politics of graffiti writing are those of anarchism."[12] As he closes his account, he notes that graffiti "stands as a sort of decentralized and decentered insubordination, a mysterious resistance to conformity and control, a stylish counterpunch to the belly of authority."[13]

In a similar spirit, Ivor Miller draws from research conducted on New York City's writing culture during the 1970s and the 1980s to argue that graffiti is an "intrinsically rebellious" public art that addresses "race" and class tensions.[14] Concerning the former, Miller suggests that graffiti

---

[9] Ibid., 47.
[10] Ibid.
[11] Austin, *Taking the Train*, 65.
[12] Ferrell, *Crimes of Style*, 172.
[13] Ibid., 197. For variations on the graffiti-as-resistance theme that take their lead from psychoanalytic perspectives, see the brief essays of Spitz, *Image and Insight*, 44, 55; and Mailer, *Faith of Graffiti*, np.
[14] Miller, *Aerosol Kingdom*, 153.

embodies a cultural critique of "the imposition of the European colonial masters' culture" upon those of non-European descent.[15] On class tensions, Miller claims that graffiti writers "combat the impositions of a consumer society" by "reshaping the alphabet to redefine their own identities and their environment."[16] Insofar as graffiti writers place their work in public, thereby making it free to consume, Miller further argues that writing culture defies a "system that put[s] a price tag on everything."[17]

Following the "cultural turn," Janice Rahn's study of graffiti in Montreal finds that it is an "adolescent obsession"[18] that speaks less to class and/or "race" tensions than to regimes of "knowledge and power."[19] For Rahn, the specific power/knowledge regimes in question are those that surround "adulthood." In this context, graffiti is said to afford adolescents an opportunity to express disdain for the normalization and disciplinary processes that can be associated with one's teenage years and presuppose the transition to adulthood.[20]

Finally, Nancy Macdonald refrains from framing graffiti writing as "resistance" by claiming that it represents a deliberate quest for social and cultural isolation. By creating a gulf between themselves and society, graffiti writers can confound and frighten outsiders—a pastime from which they supposedly derive great pleasure. As she claims: "The greatest satisfaction comes when graffiti does not just confound, it frightens. To many, graffiti is sinister and threatening and this gives writers something of an upper hand."[21] This "standing apart" and the power that graffiti writers subsequently come to possess is based on graffiti's illegality. From here, it follows that graffiti writers develop a commitment to an existence beyond the boundaries of legality and, moreover, that any attempt to move away

---

[15] Ibid., 33.
[16] Ibid., 85.
[17] Ibid., 154. For a comparable view concerning the relationship between graffiti and consumer society, see the brief analysis offered by Stewart, "Ceci Tuera Cela," 174–176.
[18] Rahn, *Painting without Permission*, 210.
[19] Ibid., 137.
[20] Ibid., 143.
[21] Macdonald, *Graffiti Subculture*, 158.

from the "illegal traditions of graffiti" would be tantamount to "taming the subculture" by opening "it up to outsiders."[22]

This brief analysis reveals the existence of numerous arguments concerning the relationship between graffiti writing culture and the society in which it is located. Yet these interpretations all emphasize illegality and suggest that the relationship between graffiti writing culture and society is defined by antagonism and conflict. For the most part, graffiti writing culture is postulated as a critical force that challenges society. But despite the tendency to emphasize the "revolutionary" or "hostile" aspects of graffiti, such approaches do not fully capture contemporary graffiti writing cultures in New York City and elsewhere.

Any discussion of post-1989 graffiti ought to begin by acknowledging that many graffiti writers paint illegally and legally, often playing both sides of the fence, so to speak.[23] Nevertheless, while there is fluidity, or movement across different types of graffiti writing, there is also a tendency to concentrate most of one's creative energy in specific ways. Moreover, and notwithstanding that it may vary over time, writers often have strong commitments to either legal or illegal graffiti. To draw out how postsubway graffiti embodies new subcultural dynamics, however, it is necessary to focus on the core ways in which contemporary graffiti is produced and practiced.

## Illegal Adaptations: "Subway Warriors" and "Street Bombing"

Whereas writers in the 1970s and the 1980s predominately used ink and spray paint to mark the insides of cars, post-1989 writers discovered that by scratching and etching[24] their names into the windows and metal panels of trains, they can ensure their work will circulate throughout the system. In the mid-1990s, it was reported that 99 % of New York City's

---

[22] Ibid., 176.
[23] MacDiarmid and Downing, "A Rough Aging Out," 609 (2012); van Loon, "Just Writing" (2014).
[24] The former is commonly known as "scratchiti" and the latter "etch" bombing. Etch bombing involves the use of an acid that burns into glass, giving it a clouded or foggy appearance. Etch cannot be washed off like regular ink or paint and produces permanent structural damage. See Fig. 2.8 from the preceding chapter.

subway fleet had windows that had been damaged in either of these ways[25] and that the Transit Authority was spending approximately $3 million a year to replace scratched or otherwise damaged windows.[26] It was also reported that as much as $60–70 million a year would be required to produce a "scratchiti-free" subway system.[27] Despite such costs, the MTA has never been inclined to retreat from its "faith" in technological solutions to such "problems."

Their initial efforts involved experimenting with scratch-resistant glass; consulting an inventor in the hopes of developing a device capable of melting glass such that the surface is reconditioned; getting in touch with NASA; and attempting to implement a "zero-tolerance" policy on scratchiti.[28] It was only recently (roughly speaking, since the late 2000s) that the MTA managed to prevent scratchiti by adding layers of removable plastic sheet to windows. However, writers have since scratched their names into subway seats and other train fixtures, thereby creating a new set of problems for the MTA.

While most writers display a strong preference for the type of subway graffiti that was predominant throughout the 1970s and the 1980s, they interpret the emergence of scratchiti and etch bombing as evidence of writing culture's resilience. As "Demer," a graffiti writer who began painting in the late 1970s, has said:

> The scratchiti itself, I think that's something that just evolved because you couldn't hit trains anymore and people were dying to put their names on a moving train.[29]

---

[25] Rein et al., "Pain in the Glass," 8 (1996).
[26] Donohue, "Losing the War," 24 (2002b).
[27] Haberman, "In Subways, Vandals," B1 (1997); Haberman, "New Vandals," B1 (1999). This is presumably a cumulative figure including the cost of materials, labor, and the revenue lost from having to take trains out of service.
[28] Haberman, "Graffiti Wars," B1 (1995); Donohue, "TA Battle Plan," 6 (2000a); Fairfield, "Meltdown in the Subways," Section 14, 6 (2000); Donohue, "Shiny New Subway," 8 (2000b); Vandam, "Clear Pane," Section 14, 10 (2004).
[29] Author's interview with DEMER.

"Ewok" and "Ezo" have expressed similar sentiments, albeit in a broader sense:

> Now you can see graffiti going into glass. They are using acid that eats the glass away. It's called etching crème and it opaques the glass... It's not really my thing, but you know, it's just the way it goes... When you push something down, it's going to pop up somewhere else.[30]

> The city will never get rid of graffiti. It's part of our culture.[31]

By no means are such views restricted to writing culture. Even those opposed to writing articulate similar understandings:

> [E]very time you get one form of vandalism under control, they turn up with another, more severe form.[32]

While some writers pursue the development of more "severe forms" of "vandalism," others refuse to concede that traditional subway graffiti is a thing of the past. Even though the general public is unlikely to ever see the work, such writers continue to enter train yards and lay-up areas to produce elaborate pieces on the sides of subway cars. Rather than reaching a general audience, what matters most to these writers is gaining recognition from one's peers, which can be assured provided one documents the work. Post-1989 subway graffiti is usually photographed, but some writers make the extra effort to produce a visual record of the entire process via video camera. The visual documentation is then shared among close friends or displayed in magazines and books, and on Internet Web sites. Sometimes, video footage is published in DVD format and sold to writers and those interested in the culture.

To make matters worse for public authorities, painting the New York City subway is perceived by many writers throughout the world as one of the "highest accomplishments" within graffiti writing culture. As such, "graffiti tourists" traveling from other countries and US cities produce a significant portion of the traditional subway

---

[30] EWOK quoted in Murray and Murray, *Broken Windows* (2002).
[31] EZO also quoted in Murray and Murray, *Broken Windows* (2002).
[32] Rick Landman, member of Community Board 1 in New York City, quoted in Lambert, "New Blight," Section 13, 6 (1994).

graffiti in question. Such tourists often take the idea of painting subway trains very seriously. In 2006, for example, the MUL crew painted a whole train, a feat that has only been accomplished on three other occasions in the history of New York City subway graffiti.[33]

Arguably a more common adaptation, many writers have returned to street graffiti and focus on "hitting" highway walls, buildings, rooftops, street fixtures, and relatively accessible subway tunnels. In terms of moving vehicles, writers focus on trucks, vans, and freight trains. For those who paint in the streets, the major incentive resides in catching the attention of passersby. New York City streets, however, are generally populated with pedestrian and vehicle traffic, which makes it difficult to produce elaborate work in such settings. For those interested in producing masterpieces, freight trains are a preferred alternative to busy streets and "high-risk" subway systems. Freight yards tend to be less secure than New York City subway trains and travel across the nation. The major problem that writers find with freights is that they tend to travel through relatively desolate areas. Furthermore, it is difficult to keep track of the work that gets done on freight trains because they travel quite extensively and according to relatively unpredictable schedules.[34]

Although street graffiti does not necessarily alter the norms and values of writing culture, it does foster innovations in the methods and techniques used to write in public space. The risk associated with producing elaborate pieces in the streets means that they are much more user-friendly for those interested in saturating the city with tags and throw-ups. But as more writers saturate the city in such a manner, standing out from the crowd becomes very difficult. It is this need to differentiate oneself from others that often works as a harbinger of new invention.

In the early 1990s, for example, "Revs" and "Cost" broke with convention and popularized alternative aesthetic options. Instead of seeking recognition for showing stylistic innovation—the path traveled by most writers—they stripped graffiti down to its bare essentials by emphasizing

---

[33] The first whole train was painted in 1976 by CAINE1, MAD 103, and FLAME1; the second in 1979 by LEE and The Fabulous Five; the third in 1988 by WANE and COD crew.

[34] For graffiti on freight trains, see Gastman, Rowland, and Sattler, *Freight Train Graffiti* (2006).

the name through clarity and repetition. They began applying stickers throughout New York City, especially to the back of pedestrian traffic signal boxes. The stickers were very basic in design and, in this regard, somewhat unremarkable. But by using stickers "Revs" and "Cost" were able to saturate the city. Stickers can be mass-produced quite easily, take seconds to put up, and, quite interestingly, when the process is witnessed it is arguably less likely to be perceived as an act of graffiti vandalism as it does not require the use of spray paint or marker.[35] The way in which "Revs" and "Cost" used stickers played a significant role in rejuvenating "street art" in New York City. Not long after a variety of creative interventions, such as the use of stencils, posters, and wheat paste, became increasingly common in the public square. Moreover, the use of stickers has subsequently become so widespread that it is now possible to speak, as Claudia Walde has done, of the emergence of an independent "sticker culture."[36]

Although allowing for a bolder aesthetic, stickers place limitations on the size a writer can make his or her name. As a result, some have developed ways to produce the clarity that stickers grant on a larger scale. The most common, and most satisfactory, solution to this dilemma is the "rollie."[37] As the name implies, a "rollie" is produced with regular household paints and roller. By throwing an extension pole into the mix, writers can paint their names in high spots that would be difficult to access otherwise. Figure 3.1 offers an example of a practice that is becoming increasingly popular. To produce these works—the high-water mark of the "rollie piece"—writers gain access to the roof of the building and then paint the piece from the top down by leaning over the building's edge.

Although obviously more time consuming than the use of stickers, if executed well a writer can achieve visibility in unprecedented ways with such works. Moreover, due to the scale and location of these pieces they are often harder to remove or paint over giving the work a greater degree of permanency.

---

[35] It seems that the use of spray paint is more likely to generate public concern than the use of instruments commonly associated with fine art, such as brushes. EMA has noticed the stigma associated with spray paint: "The fact that you are using spray cans that scares a lot of people."
[36] For more on sticker culture, see Walde, *Sticker City* (2007).
[37] Sometimes "rollie piece" or "bucket paint piece."

**Fig. 3.1** A "rollie piece" painted by "Smells" and "Cash4" from a building rooftop. Photo by Luna Park

## "Legal Eagles": Painting with Permission in New York City

Thus far, we have seen that graffiti simply shifted to new locations, deployed different aesthetics, and developed new techniques after it was squeezed out of the subway system by city authorities. But for many writers, particularly those who were entering their twenties, starting families, embarking upon careers, or those developing a stronger interest in pursuing the more elaborate forms of graffiti (i.e., "piecing"), operating outside the bounds of legality was either no longer a viable option or was rapidly losing its appeal. In the "clean train" era, a writer who wanted to produce elaborate pieces had to find a quiet, out-of-the-way spot where one was unlikely to be disturbed or seek out walls for which permission could be obtained.

Of course, writers did produce legal work in the past. However, from the early 1990s and throughout the intervening years, legal graffiti has emerged as a dominant trend within writing culture. Favored locations include the exterior sidewalls of small businesses throughout the city, large factory walls in the outer boroughs, schoolyard walls, and sometimes vans and trucks. Writers simply ask property owners if they will grant them permission to produce murals on their wall space. Some property owners flat out refuse, others are skeptical until they hear the words "we will do it for *free* if you let us paint what we want," and others welcome the artists.

Legal graffiti writers do not generally seek financial rewards from property owners and will paint for free provided they are able to retain control over the creative process. The shunning of material rewards does not necessarily reflect the belief that to exchange creative services for money somehow compromises the artist and renders what they produce "inauthentic." Rather, money is shunned because graffiti writers ultimately seek a Hegelian mutual recognition from their peers, most of whom will view the work on the Internet or in magazines after it has been documented.[38] In other words, it is not money that is necessary, but *wall space*, which affords the opportunity to paint on a scale that suits writers.

Writers soon realized that they were in a totally different creative space when painting walls. As "Nic One," a writer from the Bronx who painted his first train in 1984 and transitioned to walls in the late 1980s/the early 1990s, explains:

> Subway train graffiti was always the best. I don't want to go on record as saying that the walls were better. But walls were the next feasible thing to do. What happens artistically when you go to the wall is that you have an immense amount of time to do a piece. I can take two, three, four days—a week, a month—to do a piece on a wall. Also, on the walls you get to do your piece a fairly nice size and then if you want to add background and characters and all that stuff you could. On the train, if you wanted to do all that, you could, but your piece was constricted. On the subway train it was a rectangle. The thing about walls is they became big murals. In the early to mid-90s you had a lot of people going from one aesthetic to another because we had our way taken away from us.[39]

---

[38] These points can usefully be compared with the accounts of Snyder, *Graffiti Lives* (2009); and Halsey and Young, "Our Desires," 279–280, who report similar findings.

[39] Author's interview with NIC ONE.

Despite the difficulties associated with moving from the subways to walls,[40] many writers suggest that having the opportunity to paint with permission has helped improve the aesthetic quality of graffiti. According to "Demer" and "Bisc":

> [W]ith it being legal you have the time to sit there and really work on what you're doing, to really put the detail in it and really think about what you're doing.[41]
> We are given more time to make art that says more and is more visually interesting than a throw-up.[42]

Having documented hundreds of legal graffiti works, there is certainly something to the claim that being able to paint with permission enhances the aesthetic quality of graffiti. Much of this aesthetic development can be attributed to the production process upon which legal graffiti typically depends.

A single artist or many working in collaboration produce legal works of graffiti. The number of people who work on any given mural is determined by the size of the wall. Graffiti writers are not unlikely to acquire permission to paint on surfaces that can accommodate up to, if not in excess of, 20 artists. But more often than not 3–5 artists paint murals. The amount of time spent working on a mural varies. Artists capable of painting fast can cover relatively large walls in a single day, but sometimes walls take months to complete due to the detailed work involved. Generally speaking, however, most large-scale murals are completed over the course of 2–4 days.

Most legal graffiti works contain "pieces," which utilize highly stylized lettering to portray the tag names of artists, and a "background," which typically places the names of writers in some kind of visual setting. A work that incorporates pieces and a background is referred to as a "production." Prior to and during painting, the artists working on a mural will discuss it in great detail. The themes and concepts to be explored in the background, the composition and location of pieces, the size of imagery and

---

[40] NIC ONE, for example, also stated that he struggled to get a hold on "size proportion from 90 to 93."
[41] Author's interview with DEMER.
[42] Author's interview with BISC.

letters, the colors to be used, the style in which things are to be painted, will all be discussed and sometimes debated at length. Detailed sketches are oftentimes produced in advance and then reproduced on the wall, but more often than not artists will be accustomed to working as a group and will develop a set of creative ideas during the painting process.

That graffiti writers take their aesthetic production very seriously is further reflected in the concern they display with the materials they use. Replicating the way a "fine artist" primes a canvas, legal graffiti writers will use regular household paint to roll or "buff" the surfaces on which murals are to be produced. They may spend anywhere from $20 to $100 on the paint required to prepare a wall in this manner. To make the process of priming walls much more time efficient and less labor intensive, some have invested several hundred dollars in air compressors and spray guns.

More importantly, graffiti writers are very fussy when it comes to the aerosol spray paint cans that they use. Since the early 1990s, spray paint manufacturers have worked with writers to create aerosol cans specifically designed to suit the intricacies of graffiti painting. The first such aerosol can was released in 1994 and came to be known as "Spanish Montana." The can was instantly popular among European graffiti writers and was soon being exported around the world. Since 1994, a range of new companies, graffiti-related products, and aerosol cans have emerged. A graffiti writer can now choose from aerosol cans manufactured by companies such as "Spanish Montana," "German Montana," "Belton," "Loop," and "Ironlak," to name only a few. Aside from the well over 1,500 colors now available, arguably the most important development in terms of aerosol paint was the introduction of low-pressure cans. These aerosol cans release paint at a much slower and "softer" rate, allowing graffiti writers to shade in ways almost impossible with the paint that was available during the 1970s and the 1980s. "Loomit," a well-known writer from Germany, has worked with Belton and explains some of the intricacies involved in manufacturing spray paint that suits the needs of writers:

> It might appear very simple but it's not... The pigments must be right, it must be the right liquicy so that they don't clog the caps. [The can] must be the right pressure so they have the nice lines. So many things need to be balanced, so it takes some time. Every spray paint color has many different elements, not just the pigments. It's the thinner which keeps the color liquid, which is also the carrier for the pigment. You also have the gasses to produce the pressure to get the color out of the can... Certain quality

standards have to be met like how the line has to come out and how fast the color has to dry. Some colors are faster drying than others, but fast drying colors also usually fade pretty soon. So they have to find something that dries fast and doesn't fade.[43]

But it is not only the cans that have advanced. There is also an extensive market for the caps that dispense the paint from the spray can when pressed. Caps allow a writer to vary the width of spray. Over the last two decades, consistent advancements have been made in this area and, just when you think spray paint manufacturers had reached some kind of outer limit, they never fail to come up with something new. These days a writer can make lines almost any width he or she chooses. There are caps that create a spray pattern about the width of a pencil all the way to lines that are 12 in. wide.

Due to new antitheft technologies and savvy storeowners who know it might not be a good idea to leave paint out of view, stealing these products is difficult. A good quality can of aerosol spray paint costs approximately US$8. A cap can cost 50 cents and, given that they clog fairly easily, it is not unlikely that an artist will need to use 3–4 caps per can. This means that every high-quality can of spray paint used comes at a cost of approximately $10. Interestingly, the American paint brands that Castleman's graffiti heroes evidently valorized, and which presently cost less than half as much as the new paints, have been disavowed by legal graffiti writers. Not only do today's graffiti artists refrain from stealing their paint, they spend twice as much to work with the best materials.

These costs add up. To produce a decent piece, a legal graffiti writer will use at least five cans of paint.[44] Although it varies, the background of a legal mural will likely require another 5–10 cans of spray paint. Thus, a work of legal graffiti that includes five pieces and a detailed background can easily require several gallons of house paint and 30 cans of spray paint. In short, stealing relatively cheap American brands of spray paint and then illegally painting subway trains is no longer the dominant method for the production of graffiti. A portion of today's graffiti writers actively seek permission from property owners to *spend* approximately $350 on murals

---

[43] LOOMIT quoted in Murray and Murray, *Broken Windows* (2002).
[44] Halsey and Young, "Our Desires," 278, 290 also find that graffiti writers—even those who paint illegally—will spend approximately $50 to produce a "piece."

**Fig. 3.2** An example of a "production" featuring work by "Tone," "Hef," "KA," and "Yes1." Photo by Roman Akkerman

**Fig. 3.3** A second example of a "production" painted by "Pase," "Welin," and "Me3." Photo by Roman Akkerman

that will appear on walls they do not own. Given that graffiti writers do not own the walls, and given the public nature of these murals, it is unlikely that they will derive any direct material advantages from such paintings (Figs. 3.2 and 3.3).

## A "Respectable" Material Existence and the Embracing of Dominant Values

Contrary to popular belief, much contemporary graffiti is not produced by "youth." To be sure, and as Gregory Snyder points out,[45] many of those who currently paint with permission did start their "careers" by painting illegally at some point in their teenage years. However, as they began to

---

[45] Snyder, *Graffiti Lives* (2009).

approach adulthood and as the trains became a less viable painting option, they transitioned to legal work. Once this transition is made, they tend to remain on the permissible side of the border that divides legal from illegal graffiti. It would seem that with a steady job, mortgage payments, family, and other responsibilities, illegal graffiti quickly comes to be seen as too great a risk to one's career and lifestyle.

The graffiti writers I have interviewed range in age from 23 to 50 years of age. Although the majority of these interviewees are men, they come from a variety of class and ethnic backgrounds. Contemporary graffiti writers display great occupational diversity: I have met writers that are graduate students, corporate employees, teachers, fine artists, professional graphic designers, and many others pursuing creative careers, such as interior design. Some, ironically perhaps, work for the MTA or within various branches of law enforcement. Many of the older graffiti writers with whom I have spoken (those older than 30 years of age) are successful homeowners in the process of raising their own families. This relatively "conventional," or what one might want to call "respectable," material existence tends to be accompanied by an embracing of hegemonic values and a desire to participate in society. Perhaps the best way to demonstrate this is by directing attention toward those conversational moments during which it was particularly evident and, more pertinently, rather unexpected.

## *Opposition to Vandalism and the Genuine Concern over the Aesthetics of Public Space*

I asked my interviewees to reflect on their feelings concerning some contemporary forms of illegal graffiti, especially scratchiti and etch bombing. In asking this, I was expecting to hear a variety of rationalizations for these practices. Most of my respondents, however, voice opposition to "graffiti vandalism" and often express sympathy for owners of private property. "Been3" and "Ema" acknowledge the overall legitimacy and clarity of laws in New York City regarding illegal graffiti writing:

> The vandalism, if you get caught, you get caught man. Don't bitch and moan about it. You got caught doing something you weren't supposed to do—you painted somebody's property.[46]

---

[46] Author's interview with BEEN3.

> [I]t's against the law to write on someone's property. You don't ask for permission so you have to deal with the consequences. And that's something I'm really surprised with graffiti writers sometimes because they don't accept that. For me, each time I did illegal graffiti I accepted the fact that I am doing something that someone may not like. And if I get caught, I go to court and if I have to pay a fine, I pay the fine.[47]

"Sonic" and "Bisc" articulate an ethic of graffiti writing that involves showing respect for some forms of private property:

> [Y]ou have the new guys that are out there and they don't know what they're doing. They're writing on people's garages, they're writing on people's cars and vans and they're writing on people's gates. I don't appreciate that. If you're gonna get into graffiti, you better learn the rules of graffiti. Anything that is owned by the city—that you pay taxes for—part of that is yours. You sort of have the right to do it without anybody really getting upset about it—except the city. If a bunch of graffiti writers go and write all over the buses, you know what, we are gonna pay a little more in taxes. Who the hell is gonna notice it? We pay taxes for wars that we don't even understand...[48]
>
> I love seeing graffiti and I love the scratch shit and I love the etch. What I don't like is the fact that—being older and kind of understanding what it takes to run a business and have a window in front of your shop that costs thousands of dollars—and a 12 year old kid comes by and does an etch bath tag on it... It's a little fucked up. I think there is some systems that can afford that—like Starbucks or Wal-Mart or a big business. But you go by a barbershop—some dude put 20 years of his life into buying that place—and a little kid, ignorant to what that took, comes and vandalizes it. I think it puts a bad thing out for graffiti.[49]

Related to this self-imposed ethic, which distinguishes appropriate from inappropriate ways to paint graffiti, writers also display genuine concern for the appearance of their neighborhoods. This is often accompanied by efforts to work in ways that benefit the city and the public square. In talking about legal walls, "Been3" and "Nic One" said:

---

[47] Author's interview with EMA.
[48] Author's interview with SONIC.
[49] Author's interview with BISC.

We are not doing anything illegal. We are asking for permission. We are paying for all our own supplies, which is helping the city because we are paying taxes on it of course. Everything they need is being done: They don't have to pay to maintain [walls] because we're maintaining [them]. Also, it makes the neighborhood look better than just having it destroyed. But they don't want us here. They want to get rid of [graffiti].[50]

[W]hen you apply this art form to a bland, otherwise dull surface, it becomes more invigorating. This artwork makes anything look a thousand times better than it looked before. The only problem—because it is spray paint and because it's on the exterior of a building—is the upkeep of it. The sun beats it down, it gets withered and worn, the colors don't look as vibrant as they did the last year. But I'd rather do something new every year.[51]

In some of the above quotes, we see how writers acknowledge the legitimacy of law and are genuinely concerned with the aesthetics of public space. This respect for public space is further demonstrated in conversations about the MTA's *Art for Transit* program. After approximately 20 years of fighting subway graffiti, and any other type of unauthorized public art, the MTA now commissions artists to produce works for the subway system on a regular basis. Quite a reversal of previous policy, the idea is to brighten up what is otherwise a fairly bleak underground environment. In asking graffiti writers about the *Art for Transit* program, I was expecting to hear resentment toward the MTA for their sudden willingness to work with "conventional" artists. However, many contemporary graffiti writers voice support for public arts projects and often express an active desire to participate:

The *Art for Transit* program is cool but they are forever playing themselves and doing humanity a great disservice for not finding a balance with writers. I hope the generations that take control of these institutions aren't so ignorant.[52]

Anything that will help the public accept art more—I'm all for it. Anything like that, I'm all for it... definitely.[53]

---

[50] Author's interview with BEEN3.
[51] Author's interview with NIC ONE.
[52] Author's interview with CERN.
[53] Author's interview with DEMER.

I myself can adapt to different mediums. I could deal with something like [the *Art for Transit*] program especially if there is a little money involved or some exposure. It's just another outlet.[54]

But, as "Lady Pink"—who has appeared in almost all of the cultural media based on New York City graffiti, such as Ahearn's *Wild Style,* Silver and Chalfant's *Style Wars,* and Cooper and Chalfant's *Subway Art*—has said, the chances of writers being welcomed as participants in officially sanctioned civic culture seem unlikely at present:

RK: I'm guessing you are familiar with the MTA's *Art for Transit* program?
"Pink": Yeah, I almost submitted to the last project
RK: Can I ask how you feel about such a project?
"Pink": I think that they're offering a lot of money to get your art work up prominently on the subway system and I'm gonna go for it. I just don't think that the panelists are gonna sit there and comb through my resume... [They'll] absolutely choke at the fact that it says graffiti this and graffiti that. I've been known to get grants from the city just by my images, my background, professional skills and [art gallery] shows way back. But then you get some stuffy people who might be on the panel and just absolutely will not hear of it. They just want to look at what I did 25 years ago and call me a bad teenager.[55]

## *Seeking Social Incorporation*

For a writer to produce legal work, they must be prepared to sacrifice the anonymity that historically provided a sense of security and protection. Insofar as this exposure is for the sake of operating within the law, taking such a step may seem uncontroversial to many. But in a discursive context where graffiti remains tainted with a sense of "general lawlessness," "antisocial behavior," and so on, such a step can be read as one that presupposes a shift in consciousness. In the preceding chapter, we saw how graffiti writers were given a license to think of themselves as "artists"

---

[54] Author's interview with PART. At the time of writing, PART has been painting graffiti for over 40 years.
[55] Author's interview with PINK.

due to absorption into the art world. With the transition to legal walls in the 1990s, a similar dynamic involving the development of a new kind of consciousness once again emerged.

However, although the general dynamic is comparable there are also significant differences. Whereas in the 1970s writers were physically entering the art world, in the 1990s they were physically entering the public square. These different physical spaces are undergirded by different systems of meaning and economic significance. While one enters the art world as an artist, one enters the public square as a member of the citizenry pursuing legitimate interests. Instead of entering a relatively enclosed circle, writers were now walking among the general public. Moreover, whereas entering the art world suggests a desire to benefit economically, entering the civic community implies the willingness to volunteer without necessarily expecting monetary rewards for doing so.

That many writers have begun to see themselves and their art form as "legitimate" participants and objects within the public square can be seen in changes in their vocabulary and when asked what kind of place in society they would like to see writing culture occupy. In the train era (the 1970s and the 1980s), writers would describe their painting expeditions as "bombing," "hitting," or "killing." The pieces on trains were described in terms of how much of the train's surface was covered by the work.[56] In the 1990s, with the transition to legal walls, writers now got together to "paint." If the previous vocabulary suggested aggressive action, the new vocabulary was suggestive of a peaceful and harmless process. As noted, the final works became known as productions. While writers have a long tradition of working together, the notion of production is important insofar as it registers the ways in which they have moved away from thinking about their works in quantitative terms to qualitative terms. The notion also acknowledges the ways in which the work is now dependent on successful cooperation with people from outside the writing community, such as property owners.

---

[56] There are various ways to position your piece on a train exterior. "Panel pieces" are below the windows and between the doors; "end to ends" are works below the windows that extend the length of a subway car; "top to bottom" pieces extend from the top of the train to the bottom, but not necessarily its length; "whole cars" cover the entire side of a subway car.

When asked about the kind of place in society they would like to see writing culture occupy, writers consistently emphasize the importance of seeing it acknowledged by mainstream society. From here it often follows that writing culture should also be actively incorporated by social institutions. Many, such as "Been3," "Sonic," and "Part," have suggested a possible relationship between schools and graffiti:

> I teach and graffiti helps me with the kids. The minute they know I write, it's like: "Oh, can you do my name?" And it's like: "No, but you can do your name and I can just help you along with it." And now these kids are more into learning because I'm one of them. It's like: "Oh, he writes. He's not a regular teacher. He's a writer, man. Look at the work he does." And I bring my portfolio into work all the time. They love it.[57]
>
> I'd like to see it in schools so kids could actually learn about graffiti. Because once they learn about it in schools they're not going to want to go outside and vandalize because they know what it is. If you learn it in school you would want to do it in the positive form.[58]
>
> I would like to see it being taught in schools as a curriculum, as a study. And I would like it to be widespread, where it's an outlet. It has its format and it could be used as a useful tool in society.[59]

The desire to see writing culture recognized as a vital part of a shared cultural atmosphere is also often expressed:

> Well, I'd like to see more movies and documentaries on graffiti. This way people can learn more about it. There should be a museum on just graffiti writers based on New York and other states and countries. I mean, there is a lot of places where graffiti should be even though it's not and will probably never be.[60]
>
> I'd like to see it occupy a space in fine arts. Graffiti to move on into fine arts, absolutely, because it is that. I'd also like to see it grow in public art realms. There are those traditional mural companies that think that painting with

---

[57] Author's interview with BEEN3.
[58] Author's interview with SONIC.
[59] Author's interview with PART.
[60] Author's interview with SONIC.

brushes is the only way of creating murals. And by now we've got a 30-year tradition of painting murals around the world with spray paint.[61]

To have the first graffiti museum in New York where graffiti has originated and nobody has yet to open a graffiti museum here. Like, *I do not understand it*, you know what I mean?[62]

Of course, none of this suggests that writers do not continue to legitimate their presence within the public square by conceiving of themselves as artists. However, with the transition to legal walls, there is a new and growing sense among a large portion of writers that they embody and act as a positive presence within civic communities. This trend occurs alongside, and not necessarily in opposition to, previous methods for legitimizing one's status.

### *The Disavowal of Violence*

If writers have begun to think of themselves as part of civic communities since the 1990s, they have also begun to interact in new ways as well. The most notable change to occur in relation to the social interaction patterns among writers concerns violence, or what they refer to as "beef." Simply put, with the advent of legal walls, violence among writers has decreased. To be sure, there was never a disproportionate amount of violence within writing culture, nor has it totally subsided. Yet, when writing was more or less confined to the subways there were two major sources of tension. First, as the whole spectrum of writers—that is, from "taggers" to "style masters"—worked on the subways, there was not enough space for everyone to leave their mark. Thus, a writer often had to go over another writer and this caused problems. Second, writers often felt a need to defend yards and lay-up areas to keep inexperienced writers out. This was done to prevent the yard or lay-up from becoming "hot" (i.e., under surveillance by relevant authorities). As "Shame One" has put it:

> We [TAT (Tough Ass Team)] and TNB (The Nasty Boys) crews] locked that mutha fuckin' yard down, nobody who wasn't down with us could enter without catchin' a beat down... Now don't get the wrong idea, we were not on some gangster shit, but we had a good thing and if we would

---

[61] Author's interview with PINK.
[62] Author's interview with MERES.

have let toy rookie ass wunnabeeze come in the yard as they please, we would not have had it so good for so long.[63]

As graffiti has moved out of the subways, these spatial problems have generally been resolved. Given the effort it can take to secure legal walls, and knowing that the city is now their canvas, those invested in "tagging" have come to respect the work of muralists for the most part. Furthermore, knowing that they can paint and repaint walls for which permission has been secured, legal muralists do not need a production to last forever. In fact, "legal eagles" often repaint their walls shortly after they have been photographed. This is because most graffiti circulates, and is viewed by others, as an image and not in its original context. As it became possible to recycle space, tensions among writers decreased. This is, of course, not to deny that some types of violence still exist within writing culture. However, as "Bisc," "Ema," and "Nic One" indicate, whatever aggressive tendencies remain tend to be contained among those practicing illegal forms:

> I would say [writing culture] is definitely dominated by peace and respect. Overall it's a peaceful culture. There definitely is bombing beef and there's definitely violence. I think it exists more in the illegal world than in the legal world. When you paint walls, you have to be peaceful if you want to paint more walls and build up a network. We just want to paint and if you're an asshole, well, no one will want to paint with you.[64]
>
> Well [violence] depends on what type of graffiti you are talking about. The more it is based on the name and putting it everywhere the more there are ego issues. I think the more it goes towards bombing, the more you have problems with writers and the more towards legal the less problems.[65]
>
> [I]n the early 80s and throughout the 70s writers didn't know of each other unless they went to certain locations within the subway or they did yards and met up with each other. In the 70s the meetings was always great. In the 80s the meetings was "so so" because room on the trains was being taken away from us. Then you get to the 90s and now we got walls. Basically, a lot of beefs, and all this animosity, died. "Yo, man, I heard of

---

[63] SHAME ONE quoted in Austin, *Taking the Train*, 178.
[64] Author's interview with BISC.
[65] Author's interview with EMA.

you, peace, you're good people"—that was the type of stuff that was becoming permanent.[66]

Finally, it is worth noting that many writers tend to express strong disapproval for whatever violence does exist within writing culture. As "Juse One" and "Part" put it:

> I think beef is really stupid in general. That's just part of being an adult, learning how to resolve your conflicts without being infantile. There's a lot of really stupid people in any profession—whether you're talking about the top Wall street firm or McDonald's. With graffiti writers it's the same thing, there's a lot of knuckleheads. [But violence] has nothing to do with painting. What is fighting somebody doing for the culture? I think there is a lot of unnecessary beef. And that's basically something that I don't involve myself with.[67]
>
> You're always going to have beef. But, what are you actually beefing about? What are you actually getting violent over?[68]

## With Permission

It would seem, then, that the producers of legal graffiti lead lifestyles and hold to values that many people would consider "conventional." Many of them are career- and family-oriented individuals who spend their spare time creating paintings within the urban environment. More often than not—and, to be sure, this is a hobby that can be quite expensive—the artists absorb the costs involved in producing legal graffiti. The writers see themselves and their art as contributing to communities in ways that are beneficial and, as we will see in the next chapter, it would appear that portions of the general public are appreciative of the work that they do. As they move into the public square, all the while abiding by the law, they are increasingly coming to perceive their art as legitimate and loaded with possibilities for being incorporated in positive ways within society.

---

[66] Author's interview with NIC ONE.
[67] Author's interview with JUSE ONE.
[68] Author's interview with PART.

Among those who paint with permission, the spirit of the late 1970s and the early 1980s, insofar as this was a period in which violence was more common within writing culture, has been disavowed. Moreover, many contemporary writers do not hesitate in voicing their disapproval of whatever violent tendencies do persist among some graffiti writers. Almost needless to say, this is not the type of imagery that comes to mind when one usually thinks of "anarchists," "rebels," or those who revel in their "outlaw" status.

CHAPTER 4

# Responding to the New Graffiti Writing Culture: Broader Publics, Art Worlds, and the Sphere of Commodity Exchange

**Abstract** This chapter extends the focus on post-1989 writing culture by exploring how broader publics and cultural institutions respond to contemporary graffiti. Contrary to the claims of political elites, it suggests that much of the public appreciate some forms of graffiti, especially the elaborate and colorful murals. Alongside growing public acceptance, graffiti has managed to carve out a small, but stable space for itself in the art world and is often incorporated into advertisements. While graffiti writers appreciate the benefits of such cultural incorporation, they are also aware of the dangers of being exploited within these commercial domains. As graffiti has been incorporated by art worlds and cultural industries, it also utilizes new communication technologies to further its own interests, which has spurred the consolidation of a global community of graffiti writers.

**Keywords** Culture · Art · Exploitation · Graffiti · Urban space

The basic contours of graffiti writing culture were radically transformed over the course of the 1990s and the early twenty-first century. With the emergence of legal graffiti, many writers came to lead conventional lives and subscribe to conventional values. Shedding their anonymity, they entered the public square to make meaningful contributions to the neighborhoods in which they painted. Rather than expressing any kind of hostility or resistance toward their world, graffiti writers often strived for social and civic inclusion.

Such changes have paved the way for graffiti writing culture to enter into new kinds of relationships with the general public and some important social institutions, such as the art world and consumer culture. With each involving distinct tensions, it would hardly be possible to describe any of these relationships as straightforward or simple. While it is difficult to determine how the general public perceives graffiti, it appears that many people embrace it, especially the more elaborate and colorful forms (i.e., "productions"). Taking advantage of the fracturing and pluralization that the art world experienced in the post–World War II era,[1] it is certainly the case that graffiti writing culture has carved out a relatively stable space for itself within the fine arts. However, graffiti remains on the margins of the art world and confronts a variety of obstacles in striving to move toward more central locations. When absorbed by consumer culture, graffiti encounters several sources of tension. For example, while the aesthetic style associated with graffiti is now routinely incorporated within advertising, logo design, fashion, and so on, this by no means guarantees that writers will be the ones to reap the financial advantages from this arrangement. However, while consumer culture often uses a "graffiti look," it is also the case that graffiti is now in a position to appropriate the circuits of consumer culture. This has had the effect of consolidating a global writing community, one replete with diverse aesthetic standards and new forms of social interaction.

In an effort to trace the social response to graffiti in the clean train era, this chapter explores the relationships that have formed between writing culture and the broader public, art worlds, and consumer society in some detail. Drawing heavily from interviews conducted with writers, it shows how graffiti has thoroughly infused the world by which it is surrounded and has become a more or less permanent social and cultural fixture. This, of course, implies that much of society has come to develop a tolerance, if not acceptance, for some of writing culture's important aspects.

---

[1] See Crane, *Transformation of the Avant-garde* (1987).

## Graffiti Writers and the General Public

Although the political elite and the mass print media repeatedly assures the general public in New York City that graffiti is "bad" and "ugly," and that they ought to detest it,[2] determining how "outsiders" actually feel about writers and what they do is no easy matter. The kind of broad and disinterested polling that would be required to address this question has never been conducted. While the political elite continue to make claims concerning how graffiti is generally perceived, it may be worthwhile to consult the writers themselves, who, arguably, have more direct experience with the public. Talking to writers, one learns that there is at best limited support for the notion that New York City residents simply oppose graffiti. As "Nic One" says:

> Some people understand what we do and they love it for what it is. Some people just don't understand it and therefore they don't even want to take any steps towards trying to understand this. I've been painting at walls and somebody will walk up to me and say: "Wow, this looks great." And I'm sure every graffiti artist out there that is gonna read this will know what I'm talking about. Then you have the complete opposite end of the spectrum. People walking by and going: "What is it? What does it say? Really? That's a letter? Well, why do you want to do it here? It shouldn't be like that. You guys should paint somewhere else." You know, just don't even want to understand it. Not even try.[3]

"Been3" offers a more concrete example of opposition to graffiti among some members of the general public:

> We just painted a wall and there was a guy who lived across the street who didn't want graff in his neighborhood. There was a couple of white folks painting with us, [the property owners across the street] were like: "Go

---

[2] It will not be amiss to note here that an analysis of the relationship between contemporary graffiti writing culture and the city's political elite is absent from this chapter. This is due to the fact that the response of the political sphere, unlike most other social institutions, is decidedly unilateral and devoid of any ambiguity. As such, the peculiarities and reasons for the city's reaction, which demand separate treatment, will constitute the subject matter of the next two chapters.

[3] Author's interview with NIC ONE.

home whitey" (laughter). My boy was like "It's good to be black" (laughter). He made such a stink about it. You know what happened the next day? The whole place got buffed. I think two drops of blue paint got on his asphalt and he said: "I want somebody to pay for this asphalt to be re-done." And I'm talking about two drops. I told the guy "Get a black rusto at night and do 'ptth' 'ptth' (two squirts). That's it. It's gone and he is never gonna see it again." But he made such a stink that they had to buff the wall.[4]

Somewhat ironically perhaps, opposition to contemporary graffiti occasionally comes from those who claim to have painted subway trains at some point during the 1970s and the 1980s. Among these staunch critics, the problem is not so much that postsubway graffiti is an "eyesore" or "blight" on the community, but that it is somehow "inauthentic." Within this perspective, the subway graffiti of the 1970s and the 1980s is held up as the "gold standard." By comparison, everything else is passé and unoriginal:

> It seems to me that in New York a lot of people here pretend they were writers before. When you paint, I always have ten guys that come and say: "I used to be a writer in the 80s" and "graffiti should be like this." I remember the time when I was using a paint brush and a guy said: "It's not supposed to be like this...you're supposed to be using spray paint. You're cheating."[5]
>
> [In] the Bronx or deep Brooklyn you get: "Yo, I used to write. I used to write with DONDI." Or, "I know DONDI. You know that graffiti back then on the trains..."[6]

Yet, while it seems that some people do oppose graffiti, many seem to develop an appreciation for aspects of writing culture when they learn about it from an articulate "insider." "Meres" shared the following reflections and observations:

> When I walk people around here[7] that are interested but have no clue of what the hell anything says, and I start showing them the letters, then they

---

[4] Author's interview with BEEN3.
[5] Author's interview with EMA.
[6] Author's interview with BEEN3.
[7] "Here" refers to 5Pointz, which was a building where artists could paint legally. It was a popular tourist destination highly visible from the 7 train as it runs above

can start actually seeing letters in some of the pieces. Like: "Oh, OK, I can see how they're hiding them now." It's basically just camouflaging text. A lot of people don't have a knowledge of graffiti other than what they see in the newspaper, in the press, and on the TV. So, when they come here their ideas change. They come here and they're like: "This stuff is nice. I like this but I don't like the tagging." But before that, they hear the word graffiti and they just think tagging.[8]

At the other end of the spectrum, many writers revel in sharing stories in which the general public *embraces* legal graffiti. The following stories were retold by "Demer," "Cern," "Bisc," and "Juse," all of whom have spent many years painting with permission in the public square:

> We have never had a bad comment from the general public ever... In fact, we were doing a wall with a big demon on it and he's coming out of the ground... We didn't realize it, but this was across the street from a church. We were doing the wall and we turn around and a nun comes walking across the street. Me and "Muse" are just like: "Oh man, she's just gonna lay into us." She came over and said: "I see all your guys work around. I love it. Could I have one of your cards in case we ever need anything done?" So, that's the type of thing we get from the public.[9]
>
> I have had mostly really beautiful encounters with the public in New York City and all over the world. People are often very thankful for the work we do. They offer food, music...[10]
>
> The public has been very responsive to it... I love painting neighborhood walls because of the people that are out. Like all the little kids in the neighborhood that come up and are inspired and want to talk to you and they're playing ball in the street... And, when you paint in a neighborhood the public is the best vibe because you get to know the people in the neighborhood that you are painting in. Majority of the time it's a good response. People like it, you know. And maybe it's because we don't do bullshit—we're not bombing; we're like taking something and we're beautifying it in a sense. But I can't recall a bad time I've had from the general public. Most of the time people pull up in their cars, they look at your wall,

ground in Long Island City, Queens. MERES managed 5Pointz until it was shut down in 2013.
[8] Author's interview with MERES.
[9] Author's interview with DEMER.
[10] Author's interview with CERN.

they talk to you for a second, they honk when they're going by. It has been positive. The general response has been good with the public.[11]

You know, I've never had so much flattery in my life. I don't consider myself a talented guy or anything like that. I just do what I like to do. And the response I've gotten has been really, really positive. People that are walking by with their kids stop and they're looking and they're so interested. And they're like: "How do you guys do that? How do you make those lines? Where do you get these colors? I never seen... *That's spray paint? Get out of here. You're doing that with spray paint?*" They're blown away. And I think that's the beautiful thing about art, you can just take people to a place that they could never go to. It's a totally unique experience. I can't think of one time that somebody came up to us and said: "That's gross. I can't believe you're doing that." I've never had that happen.[12]

While each of these stories conveys a similar point, "Demer's" is especially striking. Imagine the scenario: "Demer" and his friends are painting a *demon*. Although they have no knowledge of the fact, this is taking place across the street from a church. A nun approaches them and, instead of "laying into" them as anticipated, asks for a business card. She is then politely given one. This does not help support the theory that the public finds graffiti ugly and detestable. Nor, incidentally, does it seem to lend much support to the related notion that the general public finds graffiti threatening. Provided that enough aesthetic merit is displayed, it appears that some nuns can appreciate images of demons escaping the earth's surface!

Many of my experiences in the field verify the notion that much of the public does indeed appreciate graffiti, especially when done with permission. In the previous chapter, I drew from observations to show how legal graffiti is produced and how writers function as a group. Given that these observations were taking place in public settings, they also revealed how people tended to react to graffiti writers painting in their neighborhoods. Like "Demer" and "Juse," I never had the experience of seeing anyone criticize graffiti writers as they went about doing their work.

Some people would simply ignore what was happening or take a quick glance as they walked by. Others, slightly more interested, would stop and take a few minutes to observe the process of painting before proceeding on

---

[11] Author's interview with BISC.
[12] Author's interview with JUSE ONE.

their way. While these responses did not involve interacting with graffiti writers, other passersby did. Many would offer approving compliments and support the graffiti writers for what they were doing, indicating how much they enjoyed the work. Some of the public had more specific questions for the writers. They often wondered if they were being paid to paint and/or if they were available for hire. I observed many instances in which people asked graffiti writers if they would be willing to paint portraits of friends or relatives who had passed away, if they would paint a storefront gate, or perform some other kind of commercial work. Occasionally I saw graffiti writers asked about their ability to paint certain images or visual effects, such as lightning flashes, on cars and motorcycles. Every now and then people asked if they could have the insides of their houses painted, especially "something colorful" for their child's bedroom. Toward these ends, phone numbers, business cards, and email addresses were often exchanged between writers and members of the general public.

While "business" requests generally came from adults, younger people tended to place different demands on the writers. I routinely observed, for example, individuals who appeared to be in their teenage years ask writers to sign or produce sketches in "black-books." At some of the graffiti writing events I have attended over the years, I have sometimes witnessed younger people asking writers to spray paint "tags" on t-shirts and other garments of clothing.

Many interactions with the public occurred as I went about documenting graffiti in New York City. Oftentimes, people would stop walking and wait for me to finish taking photos when they noticed that I was trying to document a wall. On several occasions, people wanted to know why I was photographing graffiti. After telling them about my project, they would sometimes offer directions to other walls in the neighborhood that had been painted by graffiti writers. On one occasion, an individual told me that if I were to walk two blocks and make a right, I would stumble upon a wall that was, apparently, "very well known." Sure enough, as I turned the corner I encountered a "production" that I had seen before: I was standing in front of the "urban wasteland" wall painted by "Rath," "Vase," "Jew," "Kerz," "Kingbee," and "Dekae," which appeared several years earlier in Jim and Karla Murray's *Broken Windows*.[13]

---

[13] Murray and Murray, *Broken Windows*, 3–4. The book contains several hundred color photographs of graffiti from New York City.

These encounters seem to suggest that portions of the general public not only appreciate graffiti, but that it may come to occupy a place of significance in their lives. Much like the relationship one may form with any other type of art, some people seem to "know" the work of graffiti writers and recall it with a sense of fondness, even pride.

## Selling Graffiti: Art Worlds and Consumer Society

If the "clean train" era is a story of aesthetic innovation, (sub)cultural change, and growing public acceptance, for many writers it is also one of expanding economic opportunities. As writers continued perfecting their craft, felt increasingly compelled by their age to start pursuing careers, and as they shed their anonymity and entered the public square, they also sought to transform their creative talents—what some might call "cultural capital"—into monetary rewards. In other words, utilizing the skill sets they acquired as graffiti writers,[14] they strived to produce objects that could generate income through their exchange in diverse market places.

Many writers have transferred graffiti onto canvas to make art objects. Alternatively, they have deliberately blurred the boundary between graffiti and graphic design. As an approach within graphic design, the "graffiti look" has found a variety of marketable applications. For example, it is routinely employed in clothing and fashion to create distinct designs for t-shirts, sweaters, sneakers, and so on; it has been used in Web site design; generated company logos; and, of course, proliferated within advertising.

To be sure, these are not entirely new developments. Writers did become involved with segments of the art world throughout the 1970s and the 1980s. Furthermore, they also began to entertain the possibility of entering the worlds of fashion and advertising during this same era. However, if one may be permitted to describe the movement of the "graffiti look" within the market place as a trickle during the 1970s, and as a stream by the 1980s, it could be said that the 1990s witnessed a flooding of sorts. In fact, as a marketable object, graffiti has assumed such diverse forms that "Juse One" describes it as in the process of becoming "a kind of dominant visual discourse."[15] With that in mind, it is worth

---

[14] For an ethnographic account that explores how writers develop careers out of their subcultural involvement with graffiti, see Snyder, *Graffiti Lives* (2009).

[15] JUSE ONE, author's interview.

exploring some of the ways in which graffiti has been commodified and how the writing community tends to evaluate the transformation of its aesthetic into a product with exchange value.

In the clean train era, many writers have continued the effort to create a space for themselves within the art world. That it is well beyond the scope of this chapter to produce a list of each show that has occurred since 1989 suggests that the writing community has, through persistence, managed to compel the kind of recognition required to establish "graffiti art" as an identifiable movement, or style, within the arts.[16] And yet it would not be inaccurate to say that if graffiti thrives anywhere, it is only at the margins of the art world. This is evident insofar as contemporary graffiti art tends to be exhibited in less established galleries that cater to smaller art markets and, presumably, to clients with limited disposable income for art. In this context, it is not surprising to find that when graffiti writers are asked to consider the relationship between art worlds and graffiti, they tend to become preoccupied with the possibilities of moving from peripheral locations to more central, and thus financially rewarding, spaces. Along these lines, writers identify several reasons for the relatively marginal status of graffiti art.

According to "Demer" and "Nic One," the most obvious problem is that not every gallery is interested in marketing graffiti art. Moreover, it can be difficult to establish connections with many segments of the art world:

> Any of the people in the gallery scene who own or run galleries, if they're in any way involved in graffiti, they're for it, they love it, they want to be involved in it, and they want it shown in their gallery. If they don't, they just won't be involved and you'll never speak to them or talk to them.[17]
>
> There are people in the art world that get it. But it's always a mixed bag. For the most part graffiti has its way of carving its own niche out in the art community. And it has because you have collectors out there that are seeking out certain names within the aerosol culture. The thing about aerosol art is that either you are going to get it and like it or you're not going to get it and you're just not going to have any connection with it.[18]

---

[16] For more on the idea of "graffiti art," see Austin, "More to See" (2010).
[17] Author's interview with DEMER.
[18] Author's interview with NIC ONE.

For others, tensions between writing culture and the art world have little to do with graffiti per se, but arise out of a much broader and general dynamic between *all kinds of artists* and the commercial nature of art worlds. In this view, the problems experienced by graffiti writers are by no means specific to them but simply reflect what any artist is likely to encounter as they strive for recognition from the art world. According to "Cey," who began writing during the 1970s and has participated in several gallery movements since then:

> I always think that artists are underpaid. Overall, artists are just always underpaid even if they are getting what they *think* they deserve.[19]

"Juse One" has made a similar point:

> It's very hard to get fair compensation as an artist period. As a graffiti artist I'm not really expecting to make a lot of money doing that. The art world is a treacherous place. The economics involved require them to come up with a sellable product. So the art world is just as much as the music world about creating something that is designed to be sold. And if it's not going to make money then it's probably not going to get made, or if it gets made it's not going to get any attention.[20]

To account for their marginal location, other writers tend to move away from the peculiarities of art worlds. Instead, they focus on what they perceive to be inherent limitations of graffiti and, in unashamed moments of brutal honesty, graffiti writers. According to "Bisc," it should hardly come as a shock to find that any attempt to sell graffiti as a cultural commodity, especially when it is more or less ubiquitous in other respects, is probably going to encounter insurmountable difficulties:

> There is an art world for graffiti—obviously—and it's big, but I don't think a lot of money moves through it. If it exists on the street it will never see what some fine art sees as far as galleries because why are you gonna pay $50,000 for a canvas when you could go look at it on the street?[21]

---

[19] Author's interview, CEY's emphasis.
[20] Author's interview.
[21] Author's interview.

On the other hand, several writers suggest that the writing community itself must take some of the responsibility for the limited space they have come to occupy within the art world. One such reason is as follows:

> The only problem I see with graffiti in galleries is that graffiti writers a lot of times tend to shoot themselves in the foot. For example, they'll be given a show and they'll fuck up by writing all over the walls in the bathroom or in the hallways or in the stairways. And they ruin what is good for them.[22]

And, finally, other respondents place less emphasis on how some writers act in order to focus on the quality of what they actually produce when within the gallery context. To quote one writer at some length:

> I would say graffiti art is very much considered an outsider art, a lower form of art. But because the art world is so market driven there is a kind of resurgence [of interest in graffiti art]. "It's the look, it's hot right now, we can sell it." One criticism I have of graffiti is that, outside of the aesthetic, I feel it's limited on what else it has to say and offer intellectually and philosophically. Can a new writer think about writing and what they want to do with it? Is it any different than a writer in the 1970s? Like graffiti on a canvas, like letters with arrows and some bubbles—everyone can do that. So what makes someone more significant? A lot of these guys all look very similar. A lot of the time it's these weird looking characters, these faces, and characters with weird hands and arms and maybe no eyes and then there will be some stenciled letters. And it's so formulaic. I know there's gonna be some drips, some splatters. And so it kind of "looks cool, kind of looks raw, kind of looks urban"; there's a little spray paint in it. But more than anything it's about, "Look at the style in which I drew it." *It's illustrative.* The artists themselves might say it's about this or that, but I really don't get that from the work.[23]

While graffiti may be the shallowest of fine arts, writing culture might take comfort in the fact that it seems to have met with greater success in an area often regarded as devoid of any intellectual and philosophical depth whatsoever: consumer society.[24] Throughout the clean train era, the

---

[22] Respondent's name withheld.
[23] Respondent's name withheld.
[24] See Adorno and Horkheimer, *Dialectic of Enlightenment* (2002); Macdonald, "A Theory of Mass Culture" (1957).

aesthetic look associated with writing culture has become common parlance within advertising, logo design, clothing design, and so on.

As early as 1993, the *New York Times* was reporting on writers being hired to paint storefronts for small businesses in the boroughs of New York City.[25] By 1995, they were reporting on a specific group of writers from the Bronx—TATS CRU—who had managed to establish a legitimate business capable of securing contracts to paint outdoor advertisements from major US companies such as Coca-Cola.[26] Since then there have been no shortages of cases in which writers have pursued legitimate economic opportunities inside the commercial sphere. To give a few examples, in 2005 *Time Magazine* created a controversy when it paid "Cope2"—a graffiti writer from the Bronx who now makes a living out of his graffiti writing—somewhere in the vicinity of $20,000 to paint a banner that would also serve as the cover for an issue of the magazine.[27] Also in 2005, Sony hired writers in seven major cities to produce outdoor ads for one of its products.[28]

But the advertising industry is far from the only commercial domain that has proven susceptible to writing culture's aesthetic. Fashion has become another major area in which graffiti has been transformed into a salable commodity. Perhaps the most well-known graffiti-inspired urban apparel wear is that created by Marc Ecko. Begun in 1993, by 2001 Ecko was reputedly making $200 million a year.[29] In 2003, Calvin Klein employed three very well-known New York City writers to supply designs for the fragrance CK One in hopes of "restoring vitality" to the product after slumps in sales.[30] Nike has collaborated with New York City writer "Futura" to design and produce a limited edition sneaker. The shoes, of which only 24 pairs exist, now fetch up

---

[25] Marriott, "Too Legit," Section 13, 4 (1993).
[26] Marcano, "TATS Cru Wins," Section 13, 4 (1995). TATS Cru has been hired by companies such as McDonald's, Sony, and BP to produce outdoor advertisements.
[27] Mooney, "Times Magazine," Section 14, 5 (2005).
[28] Richtel, "Sony Got Hip," Section C, 8 (2005).
[29] Muro, "Antidote to Pharmacy School," Section 14, 3 (2001).
[30] La Ferla, "CK One's," Section 13, 8 (2003). The writers were ESPO, FUTURA, and DELTA.

to $5,000.[31] Arguably as unforeseen, but not necessarily surprising, graffiti has been a prominent feature of several video games in recent years. The most well known of these is "Getting Up: Contents Under Pressure." In it, players overthrow corrupt political systems through graffiti writing. The game was developed in consultation with some of New York City's most well-known writers, such as "Seen UA," "Cope2," "T-Kid," "Futura," and "Smith," and includes avatars of them that are central to the player's progress. The game caused considerable controversy in various regions throughout the world; Australia even went so far as to ban it.[32]

These examples demonstrate the extent to which the borders between writing culture and the commercial sphere have become incredibly porous. They also reveal the potential of graffiti to assist in generating relatively large profits, which prompts one to consider how writers perceive the recent commodification of their art form. Previous theorists, most notably Hebdige, have argued that the absorption of independent cultural practices into the sphere of commercial exchange signifies the dissolution of their critical potential.[33] However, for many graffiti writers, the issue is not one of maintaining a position that is independent of consumer culture and therefore one from which a "resistant" standpoint can somehow be secured, but a matter of establishing *connections with* those who control capital to ensure that any possible economic advantages are distributed in an appropriate and just manner. In other words, when it comes to the commodification of graffiti, the main concern shared by graffiti writers is whether they will be the ones to reap the financial benefits from the commercial use of an aesthetic style that they are responsible for creating. As "Nic One," "Sonic," and "Demer" put it in the course of their interviews:

> I think it's a real good thing when we can get in and work with people outside of the culture. The problem with it is, as always, it's the easiest art form to be taken, mixed, molded, and reproduced without the artist getting anything. Because outside entities come into our world, our culture, they look at the way we do certain things, then they'll go pay some other people

---

[31] Martin, "New York Sneakerhead," Section 14, 4 (2004).
[32] Hutcheon, Hearn, and Braithwaite, "Australia Bans," (2006).
[33] Hebdidge, *Subculture* (1979); Hall et al., *Resistance through Rituals* (1976).

top dollar and they cut us out. You'll see a lot of computer-illustrated graphics that are graffiti based. And if you're from the graffiti world, you'll sit there and say, "a graffiti writer *had* to have something to do with that." And, yeah, a graffiti writer had something to do with that, but not necessarily created it for them.[34]

When it comes down to having real graffiti writers do these advertisements and getting paid good money for it, it's all great. I'm happy to see graffiti writers make money for it. That "sell out" stuff—forget about that. [Advertisements show that] graffiti is a part of America—a big part of America—and they use it to advertise their multi-million dollar business and their products, but yet they'll lock a graffiti writer up in a second if they actually caught him doing anything that wasn't legal. [But] for someone who never hit a wall and never did graffiti, yet actually take the style and use it and make big money of it, there's a problem there. I don't really dig that too much.[35]

When you have a graphic artist trying to imitate graffiti I think it's wrong. If graffiti writers can get paid and be involved in it, then I'm definitely all for it. People say it's "selling out," but I think that's a ridiculous term. If you love what you're doing and you can get paid to do it, there's nothing better than that. I work in an office—nine to five, corporate America—I hate it. If I could be out here painting all day and getting paid for it, and you want to call me a "sell out," no problem. No problem, because I'd be happy and I'd be paying my bills. So that term, "sell out," I think it's one of the worst terms.[36]

What these quotes reveal is that writers, aside from their general awareness of the dangers of exploitation, are also conscious of the ways in which earning an income is itself a form of not only material, but also symbolic power. Writers are arguably correct in assuming that fostering public knowledge of the ability of their creative work to generate income will be more effective in challenging negative perceptions regarding writing culture than choosing to remain at the margins of society. It is in this vain that many writers now strive to work not against, but as "Nic One" might well put it, "with people outside the culture."

---

[34] Author's interview with NIC ONE.
[35] Author's interview with SONIC.
[36] Author's interview with DEMER.

## Circulation and Globalization

When the train era ended, it was paramount that writers find new methods of circulation for broadcasting their work. As a result, they, along with some sympathetic "outsiders," intensified the use of magazines, the Internet, video/DVD, and books to document, preserve, and display the ephemeral nature of writing culture's creative output.[37] More often than not, such products are produced, distributed, and sold through independent means, but occasionally they are made in collaboration with established, and therefore economically profitable, publishing companies.

Although this latter point suggests that the appearance of graffiti in magazines and books is simply another variant of the commodification of writing culture, several closely related criteria set the present phenomenon apart. In analyzing the relationship between writing culture and consumer culture, we saw how the "graffiti look" is used to promote a wide variety of products. In the present instance, it would be more accurate to say that we are seeing the use of new technologies to promote graffiti. In this sense, it is not only that the sphere of commodity exchange uses writing culture, but that writing culture also uses the sphere of commodity exchange.

The profit motive tends to become secondary, if not irrelevant, when graffiti writing culture appropriates the commercial sphere's major communication technologies. This is arguably most evident in the extensive use of the Internet to display images of graffiti. There are now literally hundreds of Internet sites devoted to the creative output of writing culture. Most moderators of these sites do not make substantial sums of money as a result of displaying graffiti. Graffiti writers have taken to new social media, such as Instagram, Facebook, and Flickr, like bees to honey.[38] In relation to magazines, writers produce many of these independently. At best, they tend to break-even or generate minor sales profits. More often, they inevitably go under after a few issues due to the high production costs associated with the independent production of a quality glossy print magazine. DVDs and books, especially those made in collaboration with publishing companies, tend to do better in the market place. Yet even these products do not generate excessively large monetary returns

---

[37] For an extensive overview of films on graffiti, see Ross, "Graffiti Goes to the Movies" (2015). See also Ross, "American Movies," (2016).
[38] MacDowall, "#Instafame" (2016).

for their authors. In fact, James and Karla Murray, authors of *Broken Windows* and *Burning New York*, report monetary losses in producing these books despite strong sales in the market place.[39] This is because the costs of photographing graffiti—equipment, travel, printing, and so on—outweigh the financial support provided by publishers.[40]

The most salient outcome of this increasingly complex relationship, in which graffiti is both exploited by and exploits commercial channels, has clearly been the globalization of writing culture. Writers now take it for granted that stable, or relatively permanent, graffiti writing cultures can be found anywhere in the world. As some of my respondents put it:

> Graffiti is in every major city on the planet. I've never been anywhere and not seen graffiti.[41]
>
> There are very few places or countries where you will by no chance find graffiti, except probably the North and South Pole.[42]
>
> Well I'm very surprised that it has gone global. We never imagined that it would. We were just a bunch of children having fun really, kicking it in the train yards. And then look what happened. We've taken over the world, commercially and artistically.[43]

However, when it comes to evaluating how globalization has altered writing culture as an aesthetic practice, writers are not so unanimous in their views. For "Slope," a writer who began painting in 1993 and has since transitioned to the gallery world, the globalization of graffiti means that "styles are so fucking recycled."[44] "Pink," on the other hand, suggests that as writing culture spreads throughout the world its journey resembles something like an "aesthetic roller coaster":

> At first, what the Europeans did with our lettering, how they didn't understand it, it was just horrid to us. Why isn't any one teaching these people?

---

[39] Author's personal communication.
[40] Author's personal communication.
[41] Author's interview with JUSE ONE.
[42] Author's interview with MADC.
[43] Author's interview with PINK.
[44] Author's interview with SLOPE.

It's because they were learning from books. The same way we would pick some ancient hieroglyphics and just mess with them. That's what it looked like to us. They *destroyed our stuff* and we were very, very upset, yet flattered that it continued and they were trying to keep it real. And little by little those Europeans came to New York, they understood lettering better. And the direction that they have taken it in is just absolutely amazing. I think that the quality of work has grown over in Europe because people are so much more cultured. Young people are raised in knowing art; you see that in their entire lives.[45]

"Pink" emphasizes that a certain kind of social interaction needs to take place before people can master and adapt aesthetic innovations to new contexts. Several writers drew attention to the other side of this argument by stressing the implications of replacing face-to-face learning with learning that occurs via the imitation of images that can be found in magazines and on the Internet:

You have to learn in the proper order. When people learn the proper way you get better all around in the right way. Nowadays, people will go purchase these magazines, look at the elaborate stuff, and try to advance to a level when they have no understanding of a simple letter. I know some people who like to do wild style letters and can't do a block letter to save their life. How you gonna do wild pieces and you've got no structural form of a regular letter? It just amazes me, but that's the way it is.[46]

The first graffiti magazine I saw was *12 oz Prophet* and they had a [3D] production. So I saw that and I was like, "whoa, I want to do stuff like that." For [some kids] piecing is more interesting. So, this kids got dope pieces, dope burners, but can't do a hand-style to save his life. That's sad, but even I'll admit to being a part of that too. I had been painting for three or four years before I developed a consistent hand style.[47]

At the other end of the spectrum, many writers associate the globalization of graffiti with aesthetic growth. However, in these cases development was

---

[45] Author's interview.
[46] Author's interview with MERES.
[47] Author's interview with JUSE ONE.

not necessarily dependent on face-to-face interaction but occurred simply as a result of having greater visual access to a wider variety of styles:

> You can look up millions of graff pictures on the Internet. It is no problem anymore to find inspiration and information on techniques and how to construct letters.[48]
>
> Now, because time has gone on and everybody has access to it through magazines, through the Internet, people are taking it to new levels.[49]
>
> [Globalization has] helped because we get to see stuff from people that we would never ever see. The Internet is the number one influence for graff. It has made it grow in ways that your neighborhood or crew could never have done. And that's important. Growth is important. 3D pieces, c'mon, it's amazing work. Global is great. You get to travel now.[50] (See Fig. 2.5 for an example of 3D graffiti.)

Beyond aesthetic concerns, writers frequently draw attention toward the social pleasures that a global graffiti writing community seems to invite:

> Technology has really helped to unify artists all around the world. And so in a sense it has made it a smaller community and now you can connect with all these people that you never would have had an opportunity to connect with. And so in that sense I think that it has helped to bring us all together.[51]
>
> In some crazy, unexplainable way, there is this kind of unity between writers. I feel like I could go to a city where I don't know anybody and could find a couple of writers and probably have a place to stay for the night and go out in the morning and do a wall with complete strangers. Try that with a different career. I don't think watercolor painters get together and do that. I don't see sculptors just showing up at each other's doorsteps. I could be wrong, I don't know, I'm not a sculptor. But I tell you what, you show up in Germany with some spray cans and you got some skills, you'll probably have a place to stay for the night and dudes will definitely want to paint with you. As far as a global art form, it's a global community. It's like a family that stretches all over the world.[52]
>
> [Globalization] created networks for people to travel, to experience other things, and to build relationships in a realm they would never build otherwise. Like being able to go to a place like Hong Kong or Poland and

---

[48] Author's interview with MADC.
[49] Author's interview with TOO FLY.
[50] Author's interview with BEEN3.
[51] Author's interview with CEY.
[52] Author's interview with JUSE ONE.

link with people with the same interests and paint. We don't even need to speak the same language but we can paint a wall together. A lot of things don't do that.[53]

I love it because I get to travel. With graffiti you always have a good chance to meet people you would otherwise never get in contact with and you will get to know the country and its people in a very interesting, real way... It's great too because with graffiti people of very different cultures find a connection...[54]

In some cases, writers offered concrete examples of how the bond that forms between writers through shared culture is powerful enough to transcend language barriers. "Been3" and "Slope" shared the following stories:

When we were painting [the bees wall] the response was amazing from the neighbors. They loved it. They loved the colors, they loved the bees. The [neighborhood paper] even came and interviewed us. They said, "oh, we want to interview you. Can we interview those guys?" I said, "well, they speak French. They don't speak much English." He says, "well, I speak French." So I said, "well, go over there because you'd have a better conversation than I do with them." And he interviewed them and the response was awesome.[55]

I feel like I can go to any country and link up with some writers and we have a language—even if we can't speak the native language. I'll tell you a quick story. I went to Europe in 1999. One of the places I went was Prague and I didn't know anyone and couldn't speak the language. I went to this little hip-hop shop. And we were there and like, "we're artists and we're looking for writers and want to paint trains." And they're like, "oh, you want to paint trains? Talk to this guy." You could speak just a little bit of English, literally, "you want to paint trains? Come back tonight and bring all your paint." I looked at my man and was like, "we're gonna get robbed!" But we went anyway. Fuck it. We brought our shit and it was mad cool. We followed this guy, we walked forever, find this train, and we can't even really talk. We're in this other country; he takes us to the yard... And there's just this unspoken communication happening where it's like you know how to creep into a yard no matter what country you're in. And so we went in, we painted and after we were up on this hill outside of the yard, smoked a

[53] Author's interview with BISC.
[54] Author's interview with MADC.
[55] Author's interview with BEEN3.

cigarette, overlooking the trains and it was just a trip. I don't know this dude, we can't really talk, but yet there was communication happening and that's graffiti. I feel like that can happen anywhere. Like I can go anywhere, hook up with some writers, we might know mutual people, you know, it just has that factor.[56]

The ability to transcend cultural difference is of course nothing new to graffiti writing. Since its inception, it has operated as a space that welcomes—even thrives on—diversity, difference, and plurality. What the above examples show is how writing culture's tradition of eradicating boundaries that more commonly serve to divide, exclude, and hierarchically organize social groups continues to develop and grow in a globalized world. If throughout the 1970s and the 1980s writing culture generally transgressed the color line, along with class lines and, to a lesser extent, the gender line, in the new millennium it continues to engage in these kinds of transgressions. The only difference is that it now does all this on a global scale.

## Carving Out a Social Niche

By 1989, the MTA and public officials in New York City were in a position to declare, albeit after a 20-year struggle, the creation of a graffiti-free subway system. However, with the trains no longer serving as a platform for the display of graffiti, the writers simply sought new spaces in which to paint. This, in turn, led to major shifts in the organization and value structure of graffiti writing culture. While some continue to paint illegally, many have sought out legal avenues in which to pursue their craft. The emergence of legal graffiti has helped to redefine the nature of the relationships between writing culture and a variety of social domains, such as the broader public, art worlds, and consumer culture.

These relationships can be understood as ambiguous, complicated, and, ultimately, multifaceted. Graffiti writing may have found a stable foothold in the art world, for example, but it still exists on the margins; the "graffiti look" is frequently used for commercial purposes, but the writers responsible for creating this aesthetic style do not necessarily reap the benefits of such use; graffiti is exploited by, but also exploits channels of cultural

---

[56] Author's interview with SLOPE MUL.

communication. Whereas these relationships are multifaceted, the relationship that has formed between graffiti writing culture and public officials in New York City is best described as *one-dimensional*. Despite the major structural transformation of graffiti writing, the city's response, at least in its broadest outlines, has remained consistent since the early 1970s. The gap that has emerged, and continues to widen, between the contemporary realities of writing culture and official reactions to the practice warrants separate, detailed treatment.

CHAPTER 5

# The Moral Panic over Graffiti in New York City: Political Elites and the Mass Print Media

**Abstract** Despite new modes of production and growing public acceptance, political elites and much of the mass print media continue to construe graffiti as a monolithic, destructive force. Utilizing the notion of "moral panic," this chapter maps official reactions to graffiti, demonstrating how they work to construct writers as "folk devils" and legitimate disproportionate reactions to graffiti writing. Hostility against graffiti has been a mainstay of political rhetoric for over 40 years even though writing culture has drastically changed. Furthermore, the type of empirical evidence that would support such hostility is difficult to find. All of this suggests that political and economic interests fuel opposition to graffiti—a theme pursued in the sixth and final substantive chapter.

**Keywords** Moral panic · Representation · Political elite · Power · Graffiti · Media · Folk devils

For the last 40 years or so, New York City's political elite has construed graffiti writing as a monolithic and destructive force, one that invariably wreaks havoc upon the social, economic, and cultural well-being of the city. It is not surprising that this perspective gained currency throughout the 1970s and the 1980s. After all, during this time graffiti was overwhelmingly produced in an illegal manner. However, since the 1990s, and as graffiti writing culture continues to find avenues of expression that are relatively consistent with

© The Author(s) 2017
R. Kramer, *The Rise of Legal Graffiti Writing in New York and Beyond*, DOI 10.1007/978-981-10-2800-7_5

conventional social norms, such an image is radically losing (or at least should be) the plausibility it was able to take for granted in the past.

And yet public officials in New York City have remained glued to the same "party line" regarding graffiti, continuing to speak as if nothing had changed. Indeed, it would not be unfair to say that graffiti writing culture and the official representation of it are like two continents that have been drifting further and further apart over the years. That the official discourse concerning graffiti is so out of step with historical trends suggests that political leaders are not interested in understanding writing culture, but in continuing to fuel a "moral panic."

Stanley Cohen[1] initially traced the idea of moral panic through an analysis of how powerful social actors, such as the mass media and the criminal justice system, reacted to the "mods" and the "rockers," two British subcultures of the 1960s. Subsequently, Hall and colleagues[2] and Goode and Ben-Yehuda[3] offered accounts that were more abstract, essentially developing a theoretical account of moral panics. Despite their differences, these approaches are consistent in emphasizing that moral panics consist of discursive practices that profoundly misrepresent some kind of behavior, and that such negative portrayals work to legitimate disproportionate responses. As these remarks intimate, moral panics are typically steered by powerful groups and directed against those who occupy marginalized social locations. Consistent with this notion, the following chapter explores the extent to which political elites in New York City, often aided and abetted by the mass print media, have continued to define graffiti and graffiti writers in a manner that is incongruent with contemporary reality.

## "Folk Devils" and the Relentless "Signification Spiral"

According to Cohen[4] and Hall and colleagues,[5] a key ingredient of any moral panic is extremely negative portrayals of certain behaviors or events. Cohen conveyed this idea through his concept of "folk devils,"

---

[1] Cohen, *Folk Devils* (1972).
[2] Hall et al., *Policing the Crisis* (1978); Hall et al., *Resistance Through Rituals* (1976).
[3] Goode and Ben-Yehuda, *Moral Panics* (1994).
[4] Cohen, *Folk Devils* (1972).
[5] Hall et al., *Policing the Crisis* (1978).

which are created by the mass media through metaphor and symbolization. In a similar vein, Hall and colleagues[6] developed the notion of convergence, a process in which benign activities and social groups are conflated with behaviors that are more threatening. Essentially pushing relatively harmless behaviors beyond societal thresholds of tolerance, convergences facilitate the rationalization of draconian responses to those behaviors.

Antigraffiti rhetoric has consistently painted graffiti writers as folk devils and, through various convergences, construed the practice as capable of corroding Western civilization from within. In what is clearly one major discursive strategy, crusaders against graffiti routinely portray the practice as akin to animal behavior. Apparently graffiti writers are like bears that scratch and bite into trees to declare their existence to the world.[7] Not so surprisingly, writers also "use graffiti as dogs use urine to mark their territory."[8] In more extreme cases, graffiti writers are analogized to vermin and pests. Within these metaphors, they may be thought of as "rats"[9] or as "termites that need to be exterminated."[10]

At first glance, such metaphors appear to lead in very different directions. It is clear that humans accord very different kinds of recognition to dogs and bears than they do to rats and termites. Yet, while reference is made to a range of animals, each likely to arouse different emotions and sentiments, these metaphors are united insofar as they all dehumanize and therefore effectively corrode tolerance for graffiti writing. After all, dog may be "man's best friend," but the bond implied within this relationship is by no means extended to the dog's urine, which may be found more objectionable than rats and termites.

In *The Animal That Therefore I Am*, Derrida discusses a long history of Western philosophy that, using "reason" as the line of demarcation, creates a binary opposition between humans and animals. It is on the basis of this distinction that "humans" accord themselves the right to inflict a wide variety

---

[6] Ibid.
[7] Glickman, "Weekend Warrior," Section E, 33 (2000).
[8] Jochnowitz, "Manhattan Transfer," Section 6, 10 (2000).
[9] Quintanilla, "Long Scrawl," Suburban, 1 (1995).
[10] Lemire, "Frontal Attack," Suburban, 1 (2003).

of cruelties upon animals.[11] Irrespective of whether the statements of anti-graffiti crusaders are offered with conscious intent, it is difficult to see them as bearing no relationship to the discursive history described by Derrida. If anything, it is this very history from which they draw their power and therefore have significance within sociocultural contexts. In this sense, analogizing graffiti writers to animals embodies an attempt to deprive them of "reason" and, in doing so, creates openings for the "infliction of cruelties."

Like the images grounded in animal behavior, the psyche of graffiti writers is also portrayed in ways that are inconsistent. When pseudo-psychological discourse sets graffiti within its sights, writers may be seen as anything from "feeble-minded" to an "uncivil tribe" inclined to "run wild" and cause "chaos." The idea of the feeble-minded graffiti writer is often conveyed in reports that focus on repainting efforts intended to eradicate graffiti. Such reports rarely fail to mention the "eternal return" of the graffiti writer whose persistence is, in a somewhat subtle way, attributed to an inability to register new visual information embedded within the urban environment. The trope through which such sentiments are carried is extremely repetitive:

> They'll come back... But you call us and we'll come back. Somewhere along the way, they'll get the message.[12]
>
> [Shop owners] said to us: "Why bother? They'll just come back and [paint graffiti] again"... And I told them, "Yes, we'll just come back and paint over it again. They'll get the message and move on."[13]
>
> The key is consistent maintenance until vandals finally get the message.[14]

Given all this painting and repainting by both graffiti writers and those dedicated to graffiti removal, one could just as easily conclude that it is not necessarily the former who "struggle to get the message," but the latter. In any case, as graffiti writers are rarely consulted in such reports it is the antigraffiti crusaders who come to appear as "rational" and "enlightened." As such, they can safely assume the role of guardians rightfully entrusted to correct the behavior of individuals who supposedly possess "subpar" intelligence.

---

[11] Derrida, *Animal That Therefore I Am* (2008).
[12] Peggy O'Kane quoted in Bertrand, "Graffiti-Busters," Suburban, 3 (1995).
[13] Mary Anderson quoted in Bertrand, "Flushing Strip," Suburban, 4 (2003).
[14] Julie Story quoted in Ogawa, "Graffiti Busters," Suburban, 4 (2005).

As a group, graffiti writers have often been portrayed as an "uncivilized tribe" with a tendency to act in a "wild" manner. We may be told, for example, that "graffiti vandals ran wild last year"[15] or that they went on a "rampage over the weekend."[16] Drawing from contemporary, albeit faulty, understandings of historical civilizations may evoke the same image. One journalist in particular has made a habit of referring to graffiti writers as "Visigoths" *and* "Vandals"—as if there were no significant differences between the two groups—noteworthy only for their "sacking of Rome."[17] Never let historical accuracy meddle with the rights of a powerful metaphor! Echoing the kind of critique that Stanley Cohen made of the ways in which the mass media spoke of the "mods" and the "rockers,"[18] one can only wonder if such reporting, and the people consuming it, can correctly identify the meanings of the words being used. In what sense, for example, have graffiti writers ever "sacked" (i.e., *robbed or made off with property through the use of direct force*) a city?

The animalizing and psychologizing of graffiti writers ultimately pushes them well beyond the thresholds of "normality" and "appropriate behavior." Positioned as such, graffiti writers are seen as lacking reason and the ability to exercise self-control. To put it in Freudian terms, as having somehow eluded the repression of the instincts supposedly required for entering "civilization."[19] However, the most common and powerful trope used to push graffiti into the realm of the "socially intolerable" involves drawing erroneous links between writing culture and violent forms of criminality.

One such image suggests that despite the disparity between misdemeanors and felonies, the proclivity to commit either type of offense will be found within the same "soul." The notion of a soul that harbors a broad spectrum of criminality—*Homo Criminalis*, as Foucault might have put it—is often conveyed allegorically. In an article looking at a series of crimes committed in one particular neighborhood in New York City, for example, we are initially told about the "savage" beating of a transit police officer, the

---

[15] Woodberry Jr., "Corp. Wins," Suburban, 1 (2000).
[16] Bertrand, "Tough Justice," Suburban, 1 (2004).
[17] Haberman, "Graffiti 'Art'?" B1; Haberman, "Graffiti Wars," B1; Haberman, "Vandals Etch," B1.
[18] Cohen, *Folk Devils*, 32.
[19] Freud, *Civilization and its Discontents* (1961).

beating of an immigrant "to death with boards and pipes," the "pummeling" of several navy officers, and a stabbing "outside a bar." We are also told about an act of arson in which a park building was burnt "to the ground." These crimes are then attributed to several youth groups within the neighborhood who, when a little less preoccupied with beating people to death, "seem to be mostly interested in drinking beer, occasional smoking of marijuana" and "scribbling graffiti." Although no actual evidence is supplied, park authorities assure us that the torching of the park building was committed by a group of teenagers angered by the fact that "the graffiti they inscribed on the park house was repeatedly being blotted out."[20]

When allegory and speculation are not used to convey the aloof idea of a criminal soul, inaccurate language will be favored. The convergence most commonly used to make it seem as though there is no difference between graffiti writing and criminal activity of a more menacing nature works by erasing the distinction between *writing culture* and *gangs*. More specifically, this is accomplished by failing to acknowledge the differences between "crews" and "gangs." One article, for example, informs the public of "the *elaborate designs* of gangs—which are also called posses and crews."[21] This statement is false in more ways than one. First, the notion of "elaborate designs" is clearly intended to evoke what is known among graffiti writers as a "piece." Gangs, however, do not routinely produce pieces. Thus, what the first part of this statement does is take a practice from graffiti writing culture—"piecing"—and label it as something produced by gangs. Second, although some gangs may refer to themselves as "posses," they do not refer to themselves as "crews." The obverse of this is just as true: graffiti writing "crews" do not refer to themselves as "gangs." The two cultural groupings are distinct entities, each possessing a unique historical lineage and engaging in different practices.[22]

[20] Kleinfield, "Bay Ridge," B2.
[21] Brenner, "Combating the Spread" (1993).
[22] The sloppy use of a term as value-laden as "gang" to inform the public about graffiti writing culture is not uncommon. See, for example, the following articles Hanley, "Police Squad," B6 (1995); Bayliss, "Museum," Section 2, 26 (2004); Ferris, "Graffiti as Art," Section 14WC, 1 (2002); Rein et al., "Pain in the Glass," 8. All of these articles erroneously conflate graffiti writing culture and gangs. See especially Olmeda, "Tide Turns," Suburban, 39, in which the Zulu Nation is labeled a "street gang" (1995).

It is worth pointing out that graffiti writers draw a clear distinction between "gangs" and "crews." The following remarks made by "Juse One" and "Meres"—writers who have been involved with graffiti writing culture since their early teenage years and who have no connection to gang cultures whatsoever—are indicative:

> Graffiti is definitely the most misrepresented form of art. They [mass media, political elites] take it out of context and connect it with gang violence. And, you know, there is a completely different group of people that write gang signs on walls. That has nothing to do with me going out with a crew to paint a mural. It's just not the same thing. The two things have nothing to do with each other but that's what they do; they connect things that aren't connected.[23]
>
> They [mass-media] associate graffiti with gangs a lot. It's bullshit. They are called graffiti "crews" and they're just groups of kids that are friends and they paint. It's not as bad as they like to make it seem.[24]

Despite flying in the face of what would be regarded as common knowledge among the graffiti writing community, some reports unabashedly claim that graffiti writers are becoming more "gang-like" and that one of the signs of this is a supposedly new inclination to act in a violent manner. We may be told about "ego-driven graffiti scribblers" who have "turned to violence" and now refer to themselves as "tag bangers."[25] Or about young graffiti writers who "carry a spray can in one hand [and] a gun in the other."[26] Apparently, "tag bangers" may be young, or even "little tiny kids," but we must not be deceived about the threat they present. As one transit officer informs us: "I always loosen the holster strap on my gun before I move in [to arrest graffiti writers]. You never know what is going to happen these days."[27]

---

[23] Author's interview with JUSE ONE.
[24] Author's interview with MERES.
[25] Ayres Jr., "City of Graffiti," Section 1, 20 (1994).
[26] Terry, "Graffiti-Scarred Areas," A18 (2000).
[27] Ayres Jr., "City of Graffiti," Section 1, 20.

## Limits to "Broken Windows," or the Epistemic Foundation to Demonization

The kinds of overly emotive portrayals within the mass media and political rhetoric are consistent with the emphasis that moral panic theory places on misrepresentation and negative symbolization. However, according to Goode and Ben-Yehuda,[28] the concept of moral panic rests on disproportionality, which can be said to exist when the official response to an activity is excessive in light of available evidence concerning the objective harm caused by that activity. Since its rise to prominence in the late 1970s and the early 1980s, the broken windows theory has provided much of the epistemic foundation for the practical antigraffiti efforts orchestrated by officials in New York City. As is well known, this thesis asserts that minor forms of disorder, if left unchecked, will invite serious crime and that this will eventually lead to urban decline. However, despite all the political faith in broken windows, the thesis remains surrounded by uncertainty.

Aside from the many contradictions within political rhetoric that suggest broken windows lacks plausibility,[29] sociologists and criminologists have consistently undermined the thesis. At one end of the spectrum, some researchers have found *no empirical support* for the notion that "disorder" leads to serious crime.[30] Others have found, at best, limited support for broken windows. In his study of Baltimore neighborhoods, Taylor found that some indicators for broken windows correlate with "citizen fear" and three violent crime categories (homicide, rape, and assault). His results, however, ultimately indicate that the structural variables of "racial composition" and "neighborhood economic status" perform more consistently in explaining much of the variation in disorder *and crime*.[31]

Peter K.B. St. Jean[32] also explores the problem in his ethnographic study of neighborhoods in Chicago. Beginning with evidence showing

---

[28] Goode and Ben-Yehuda, *Moral Panics* (1994).
[29] Kramer, "Political Elites" (2012); Kramer, "Moral Panics and Urban Growth" (2010).
[30] Harcourt, "Reflecting on the Subject" (1998); Harcourt, *Illusion of Order* (2001); Harcourt and Ludwig, "Broken Windows" (2006).
[31] Taylor, *Breaking Away*, 185, 231 (2001).
[32] St. Jean, *Pockets of* Crime (2007).

that within high-crime neighborhoods crime is concentrated on specific blocks, he asks why criminals choose "*this* particular block over *that* particular block?" In answering this, he turns to those who actually break the law. St. Jean finds that criminals ultimately read urban environments in terms of their "ecological advantages" for crime commission. Someone who commits robberies, for example, will privilege locations with ATMs and easy escape routes; drug dealers will approach space like any other commercial entrepreneur, focusing on convenience of location (can buyers come and go easily) and presence of diverse activities (if police come, is there another valid reason to be in this area?). The presence of things like graffiti and abandoned buildings occupy a very minor place, if any, in such calculations.[33]

Claiming that it will resolve urban problems, advocates of broken windows also assert that police should rigorously enforce ordinances crafted to regulate minor signs of disorder. The merits of such an approach are often illustrated by citing cases (especially those that occurred during the 1990s) in which cities have "cracked down" on disorder and witnessed drops in the volume of serious crime. However, with researchers pointing to a variety of alternative explanations for shifts in serious crime, such claims have not fared well in the academic literature.

According to Sampson and Raudenbush,[34] it is not the reparation of broken windows that provides a safeguard against crime, but "collective efficacy." Collective efficacy suggests that a community, insofar as they work together to solve problems, develops a sense of cohesiveness, and it is this mutual trust and group-belonging that provides a defense against criminal activity. In the more conventional quantitative approach of Harcourt and Ludwig,[35] variables such as the stabilization of crack markets and broader economic trends are identified as affecting crime rates during the 1990s. Other scholars, such as Corman and Mocan, acknowledge that economic factors do have a significant effect on serious crime, but that policing and arrests are also significant. Their analysis, however, explores the role of "felony arrests" and "misdemeanor arrests" (their indicator for broken windows policing). Importantly, they find that the

---

[33] Ibid., 149–165, 98–148
[34] Sampson and Raudenbush, "Systematic Social Observation" (1999).
[35] Harcourt and Ludwig, "Broken Windows" (2006).

former has the most explanatory power in relation to *all seven serious crime categories* and that while there is a relationship between "misdemeanor arrests" and decreases in robbery, motor-vehicle theft, and grand larceny, the magnitude of this effect is not great.[36] Taylor has ultimately reached a similar conclusion. As he puts it, "*crime fighting* [i.e., pursuing felons] *may be more important than grime fighting for long-term neighborhood preservation.*"[37]

Somewhat ironically perhaps, it is worth noting that one need not necessarily consult the critical literature to discover the limits of the broken window theory. Major proponents of the idea, such as Kelling and Bratton, admit as much in their own accounts. For example, after celebrating the eradication of graffiti in the New York City subway system, they go on to say:

> Yet, despite this achievement, the frightening and intimidating behavior of a large group of miscreants overmatched whatever advantages accrued from graffiti elimination... Robberies of passengers were increasing.[38]

This admission is quite startling. In this context, it is important to recall that "graffiti elimination" was touted as an important mission that would save the city, one that took two decades to accomplish.[39] And yet, it was, apparently, quite simply "overmatched." If the broken window theory were correct, a statement such as this would be impossible to make: at least *some* fear and crime reduction should have followed the eradication of graffiti. Finally, it may be worthwhile to point out that James Q. Wilson— a coauthor of broken windows—has openly acknowledged that the thesis was not based on any empirical data. As he has put it, while "God knows what the truth is," among us mere mortals the theory remains a "speculation."[40]

---

[36] Corman and Mocan, "Carrots, Sticks," 262–263 (2005).

[37] Taylor, *Breaking Away*, 372 (emphasis in original). For an implicit critique of broken windows from a policing point of view, see also Ross and Wright, "Better Things to Worry About" (2014).

[38] Kelling and Bratton, "Declining Crime Rates," 1221.

[39] Austin, *Taking the Train* (2001); Kramer, "Social History" (2009).

[40] James Q. Wilson quoted in Cohen, "Pie Chart is Half-Baked," B7; and Hurley, "Scientists at Work," F1; respectively.

## CAMPAIGNS OF ANNIHILATION I: TECHNOLOGY FETISHISM AND THE IMPRISONMENT TURN

That graffiti is rendered a force of such sinister proportions, and that this occurs in the absence of compelling evidence, would be somewhat comical were it not for the relatively serious consequences which accompany it. Alongside the millions of dollars spent each year on combatting graffiti, the excessive response to the phenomenon is evident in new policing strategies and the growing intensity of punishment for graffiti writing.

Reflecting the long-standing and seemingly unshakable faith in the power of technology to address "problems," catching graffiti writers took a "high-tech" turn during the 1990s. To be sure, police still "stake-out" graffiti "hot spots"[41] and they still gather as much data as possible to create extensive dossiers on graffiti writers.[42] But this kind of police work is increasingly supplemented by the use of technologies originally created for *military* purposes. For example, the police have turned to "ocular aids" that are much more sophisticated than the now commonplace surveillance camera and closed circuit television.[43] Taking their lead from soldiers fighting in the Persian Gulf War, the police began experimenting with night vision goggles in the early 1990s. With the goggles, the police hoped that they would be able to creep up on graffiti writers painting trains in darkened subway tunnels.[44] The relatively short range of the goggles, however, meant that their use was limited. While they may have been effective in subway tunnels, they did little to assist the battle against those painting graffiti above ground. What was demanded on this front was an extended range of vision. Faced with such a dilemma, the police introduced the use of night vision telescopes and other long-range video and audio equipment.[45] Armed with such

---

[41] See Quintanilla, "Long Scrawl," Suburban, 1; for police officers who staked out a train station for several weeks to apprehend a man who was drawing "lewd" pictures on the station's walls.

[42] Sclafani, "NYPD's Can-Do War," p. 19 (2005a).

[43] The MTA spent $1.1 million installing CCTV on its buses to fight scratchiti. See Rutenberg, "Camera Plan," 9 (1998).

[44] James, "Goggles Brighten," B2 (1992); Bennet, "New Arsenal," Section 4, 2.

[45] Hernandez, "Police Scope," Section 13, 12 (1993); Krauss, "Decoding Graffiti," B1 (1996).

technology, the police could stake out—usually from several blocks away—publicly visible surfaces, such as storefronts, upon which graffiti writers write their names.

Yet, for all their technological sophistication, night vision goggles and long-range telescopes can only enhance the natural capabilities of the human eye. In an attempt to transcend that human organ of surveillance altogether, the police have turned to thermal imaging technology. Such technology enables a kind of seeing not unlikely to be associated in the popular imagination with fictional characters such as Superman or the Predator. Thermal imaging cameras, initially developed by the military for battle and costing somewhere in the vicinity of $13,000 for a single unit, detect and register heat emanating from bodies. This effectively allows police officers to see graffiti writers even if the latter are located behind solid physical structures. The thermal imaging technology now being used is so sophisticated that it can detect where people have recently walked or placed their hands by the traces of heat left behind.[46]

As the New York Police Department's (NYPD's) vandal squad—consisting of 76 police officers[47] and, evidently, an arsenal of gadgets from the military—continues to arrest writers, New York City's public officials have increasingly come to perceive imprisonment as an appropriate punishment for graffiti. The idea of sentencing graffiti writers to prison can be attributed to Mayor Koch. During the early 1980s, it was he who recommended that a person convicted three times for writing graffiti be sentenced to 5 days in prison.[48] However, only recently has this idea entered the realm of practice as judges have come under growing pressure from the print media, political elites, and community groups to impose prison sentences upon graffiti writers.

While in Singapore in 1994, US teenager Michael Fay was found guilty of spray painting cars. He was sentenced to 4 months in prison, a $2,000 fine, and "six lashes of a bamboo-like cane."[49] While the *New York Times*

---

[46] Donohue, "Turning up the Heat," 17 (2001).
[47] Kelly, "NYPD Strategic Approach" (2005).
[48] See Silver and Chalfant, *Style Wars* (1983).
[49] Editorial, "Flogging in Singapore," Section 1, 18 (1994); See also Safire, "Crime in Singapore," A27 (1994).

(and much of the US mass print media) denounced Singapore's use of corporal punishment, more importantly in this context, they used the incident to portray the methods of punishment practiced in the USA— even the death penalty—as "civilized" and "humane." As one journalist put it:

> The only civilized punishment is loss of property (a fine) and/or loss of freedom (a jail sentence). Taking away a convict's freedom punishes but does not inflict pain. What about our death penalty? Not germane; that retributive justice by lethal injection is painless.[50]

As this passage makes clear, it is the supposed absence of physical pain that allows the use of imprisonment to appear as an "enlightened" form of punishment for most, if not all, crimes. Indeed, while the *New York Times* displayed no hesitation when it came to elucidating how painful Michael Fay's caning would be, they never seriously stopped to consider whether 4 months in prison could in any way be construed as an exorbitant punishment for writing graffiti.

When "Cost" was arrested for graffiti vandalism and appeared in court in 1995, one councilperson wrote the judge hearing the case a 2-page letter urging that he be sentenced to prison. When the case was being heard, local council members and members of community groups attended wearing badges denouncing graffiti.[51] Although "Cost" escaped the prosecutor's recommended sentence of 60 days in jail, he was sentenced to 3 years probation, $2,180 in fines, psychological counseling, and, finally, 200 days of community service, which was to be spent removing graffiti.[52]

"Desa," arrested several years before "Cost" and just after the Fay incident, was not so lucky. When word got out that he was arrested and would be appearing in court, a "court watchers" group quickly formed. Consisting of approximately 30 members from a variety of civic associations, the group attended every one of his court proceedings and had every intention of flooding the courtroom on his day of sentencing.[53] Dubbed the "$1 million

---

[50] Safire, "Crime in Singapore," A27.
[51] Belluck, "Graffiti Maker," B3 (1995).
[52] Ibid.
[53] Onishi, "All He Wrote," Section 13, 10 (1994).

vandal" by law enforcement officials, "Desa" was sentenced to 1–3 years in prison.[54] After serving 4 months in prison and 8 months in a work release program, he was paroled toward the end of 1995.[55]

Upon hearing of "Kiko's" arrest, a City Councilperson known for his dislike of graffiti went to the print media and not only denounced him as a "punk," but labeled him one of the "most wanted graffiti vandals." Applying such a label to "Kiko" was, to put it mildly, quite odd. While "Desa" was certainly one of New York City's more prolific and therefore notorious writers, thereby garnering him a spot in the Vandal Squad's "most wanted" list of "graffiti vandals," "Kiko" was not a name that appeared with much frequency in the public square. A journalist once tracked down and asked Steve Mona, a retired lieutenant who spent the last 10 years of his career as the head of the Vandals Task Force, about "Kiko." Mona replied by saying that he had "never heard of him."[56] Despite "Kiko" being a very minor player within graffiti writing culture, after the aforementioned city council member pressured the district attorney handling the case to push for a prison sentence, and after he insisted—despite the judge's objections—upon reading a victim impact statement before the court on sentencing day, "Kiko" was sent to Rikers Island for 6 months, put on probation for 5 years, and fined $25,000.[57]

### CAMPAIGNS OF ANNIHILATION II: ERADICATING GRAFFITI AS AN *AESTHETIC* CATEGORY

Taking on a life of its own, disproportionate reactions to graffiti have extended well beyond those who paint without permission. Since the early 1990s, the city has embarked upon a quest to eradicate graffiti as an *aesthetic* category. Not content with condemnations of legal graffiti, the city opposes commercial uses of the "graffiti look." Moreover, public officials are striving to identify and implement mechanisms that penalize

---

[54] Kocieniewski, "New Canvas," B2 (1996); Donohue, Marzulli, and Jamieson, "New Brush," 6 (1996); Donohue, "Graffiti King Back," 10 (2002a).
[55] Donohue, Marzulli, and Jamieson, "New Brush," 6.
[56] Gardiner, "KIKO Was Here," 16 (2007).
[57] Ibid.

those who can be held responsible for the presence of graffiti or those who refuse to adopt the city's hostile antigraffiti standpoint.

Political elites, for instance, have openly criticized places such as "5Pointz," which was one of the few places in New York City where graffiti writers could paint with permission. It was a relatively large warehouse building located in Long Island City, a neighborhood of Queens, but was whitewashed and shut down in late 2013 as the neighborhood continues to undergo gentrification.[58] Instead of seeing it as a place where individuals could express themselves freely and legally, or as a place that provided an outlet for those who might otherwise write graffiti in an illegal manner, one public official condemned "5Pointz" as a place that feeds the "addictions of young 'graffiti vandals,'"[59] and suggested that allowing people to paint with permission is the equivalent of "sending candy thieves to work in a candy factory."[60]

Similarly, public officials have expressed strong opposition to commercial uses of graffiti (e.g., hiring graffiti writers to paint store billboards; using graffiti-style aesthetics in advertising). Such opposition is usually based on the idea that illegal graffiti will somehow be promoted if graffiti's aesthetic qualities are incorporated into otherwise legitimate enterprises. As one police officer has said of "graffiti for hire":

> We discourage it … if graffiti, even done with permission, is tolerated in one place, it tends to spread to other places where it is unwelcome. If people want to do some advertising, let them get a billboard.[61]

This form of reasoning suffers not only from the fact that no concrete evidence is supplied to support it, but that it simply mimics the fallacious logic often used to legitimate other attempts at censorship, such as those that seek to curtail the content of some popular music.[62] More importantly, in blurring the boundary between graffiti as an *aesthetic* category

---

[58] Buckley and Santora, "Night Falls," (2013).
[59] Weir, "Patron of Graffiti," Section 14, 10 (1998).
[60] Ruiz, "Graffiti Phactory," Suburban, 4 (1998).
[61] Police officer quoted in Marriott, "Too Legit," Section 9, 8. See Assistant Chief James Tuller's remarks in Lemire, "Wiping Out Graffiti," Suburban, 3 (2002b).
[62] Wright, "I'd Sell You Suicide" (2000).

and graffiti as a *legal* category, it provides a rationale for those in the business of law enforcement to actively police graffiti not on legal, but on aesthetic grounds. Many graffiti writers who paint with permission have shared stories that verify this point:

> [The police] have run in artists that I know who have been standing in the street with permission papers [allowing them to paint]. And they're like: "No, no, we'll take you to jail and we'll see by Monday if these permission papers are real or not." The Vandal Squad have gone so far as to get into my house. They made off with over 4000 photos, took 6000 slides, all kinds of memorabilia. They didn't file any charges—they just took all my shit.
>
> We were painting uptown in the Bronx, Hunts Point. It's a community area and it was an event of all women graffiti artists. We had this whole legal wall. We were working with the BAED center and then these health officials from the department came over to harass us and told us to put our paint away. Meanwhile there is garbage piled in mountains destroying the water in the area and they can't go out and fuck around with those people.[63]

By no means should it be assumed that only writers are likely to be targeted by efforts to repress the aesthetics of graffiti. It would appear that anyone who employs graffiti writers, or embraces the visual languages they have created, can expect to find themselves castigated in one way or another. In the late summer of 2005, Marc Ecko, a fashion designer known for embracing graffiti writing culture, acquired permission from community leaders in Chelsea to host a daylong public event. Featuring mock subway cars as canvasses to be painted during the day, the purpose of the event was to showcase the talents of approximately 20 renowned graffiti artists from New York City. Upon becoming aware of the event, those at the political forefront of opposition to graffiti, such as Bloomberg and his trusted sidekick Peter Vallone Jr., successfully pressured the Office of Community Affairs to rescind the permit.[64] Not prepared to have the

---

[63] The quotes are from interviews with different graffiti writers. The print media have also reported incidents in which well-known graffiti writers, such as TATS CRU, were arrested while producing legal graffiti. See Barnes, "Mural Painters," B3 (2000). For the arrest of OVIE while painting with permission, see Gonzalez, "Legal Graffiti?" B1 (1996).

[64] Melago, "Pol Sees Red," 6 (2005b); Rutenberg, "City Revokes," B5 (2005); Lombardi, "Graffiti Party Permit," 2 (2005).

event shut down, and arguing that canceling the permit violated First Amendment rights to free expression, Ecko took the city to court.[65]

In federal court, the city was quick to rehearse the kinds of arguments against "legal graffiti" already noted. Somewhat strangely, however, they situated such claims in the context of "terrorism." This led to the bizarre suggestion that legal graffiti was a problem not only because it would encourage others to produce illegal graffiti, but also because this graffiti might "blot out" subway windows such that "people can't see what risks are out there."[66] One may be inclined to wonder whether the city's devotion to suppressing a legal event that happens to incorporate the aesthetics of graffiti embodies a rational response to the idea that serious "risks" are "out there" awaiting as you exit the train. While the federal judge hearing the case, Jed S. Rakoff, did not make this point, he did expose the absurdity of the city's position:

> By the same token, presumably, a street performance of *Hamlet* would be tantamount to encouraging revenge murder. As for a street performance of *Oedipus Rex*, don't even think about.[67]

A second prominent example of aggressively articulated opposition to "legal graffiti" is worth noting. When *Time Magazine* decided to rehash the now passé debate over whether graffiti is "art" or "vandalism," it paid graffiti writer "Cope2" $20,000 to paint a large billboard advertisement for the magazine.[68] The billboard was placed at the corner of Houston Street and Wooster Street in Manhattan's SoHo area. Even though no law had been broken, antigraffiti crusading politicians simply could not resist publicly condemning both *Time* and "Cope2" for their legitimate use of a graffiti aesthetic. As the same city council person who lobbied for "Kiko's"

---

[65] Peterson, "Ecko Designs," 14 (2005a).
[66] Paula Van Meter, a lawyer for the City of New York, quoted in Preston, "Graffiti-Themed Event," B3 (2005). So much for preserving the image of the subway as a place where one will not encounter "rampant criminality."
[67] Tavernise, "Citing 1st Amendment," B1 (2005). See also Peterson, "Party Is On!" 7 (2005b).
[68] Mooney, "*Time Magazine*," Section 14, 5.

imprisonment put it: "*Time* magazine should have spent its money rewarding legitimate artists, not some punk [who has] been defacing our city."[69]

Alongside this kind of condemnation, the city has also turned to penalizing owners of private property who fail to remove graffiti from their buildings. The logic underpinning the aesthetic control of private property seems to be that property owners should be punished for failing to support the city in its mission to deny anyone and everyone the possibility of encountering graffiti within the urban environment. In December of 2005, Bloomberg announced the passing of a new law in a press release:

> Commercial property owners and owners of residential properties... will face a fine of up to $300 for failure to remove graffiti. These property owners will not face any penalty if they inform the City—through 311—of the graffiti on their property and sign a waiver allowing the city to clean it.[70]

This statement creates the erroneous impression that property owners have only two options: they can leave graffiti up and receive a fine; alternatively, they can prevent the city's infrastructure of social control from aggressively siphoning that $300 from their hip pocket by signing a waiver that hands the "aesthetic rights" to their property over to the city.

However, property owners do have a third option. In the legislation passed, "graffiti" is defined as:

> [Any] letter, word, name, number, symbol, slogan, message, drawing, picture, writing, or other mark of any kind visible to the public from a public place that is drawn, painted, chiseled, scratched... that is *not consented to by the owner* of the commercial building or residential building.[71]

According to this definition, property owners have the option of avoiding any form of punishment by simply declaring that any "letter, word, drawing, picture" (etc.) that is visible to the public has been placed on their

---

[69] Peter Vallone Jr. quoted in Melago, "Riled Pol," 23 (2005a). See also McDonell, "Graffiti War," 47 (2005).
[70] Bloomberg Files, "Legislation to Fight Graffiti" (2005c).
[71] Section 10-117.3 of the Administrative Code of the City of New York. Emphasis added.

property with consent. While this suggests that the law is effectively useless insofar as it affords property owners an easily exploitable "loophole," to leave the matter here would be to miss the point.

That the law may be ineffective does not negate the fact that its main objective is to exercise a certain kind of power over property owners. Somewhat paradoxically, exercising the kind of power in question is partially legitimated by the notion that private property is, to borrow Durkheim's sense of the term, *sacred*—not to be "touched" or interfered with. As Bloomberg once put it in no uncertain terms:

> You do not have the right to go up to somebody's private property who doesn't want you there and exercise some mythical right of self-expression.[72]

And, in a slightly more concise version:

> You don't have a right to walk up to somebody else's property and deface it.[73]

However, as the piece of legislation in question makes unmistakably clear, when the supposedly sacred nature of property is inscribed into law it ensures that some people do end up possessing the power to exercise a "mythical right of self-expression." Initially postulated as something that nonowners are not to interfere with, this law reconceives private property as state property. Once framed as such, it is not necessarily protected from graffiti but simply exposed to the kinds of defacement preferred by those in authority.[74]

## The Grip of a Moral Panic

Scholars generally agree that discursive hostility and disproportionate reactions are the key indicators of a moral panic. In the case of graffiti writing in New York City, it is readily apparent that both of these

---

[72] Bloomberg quoted in Saul, "Mike Vows," Suburban, 1 (2002).
[73] Bloomberg quoted in Saul, "Graffiti Bust," 38 (2003).
[74] The kinds of defacement currently preferred by the city seem to be limited to ensuring that building exteriors assume a uniform veneer of "Mission Brown," "Franklin Buff," or "Tioga Gray." Alternatively, the city seems intent on defacing buildings with large, slightly mismatched patches of color.

conditions are met, if not radically surpassed. In fact, the kinds of hostility directed toward those who write graffiti in the public spaces of New York City are so extensive and multifaceted that it would be quite easy to fill several chapters mapping these in detail.

Despite the relatively innocuous nature of graffiti (not to mention the rise of legal graffiti), writers are often portrayed as animals compelled to follow "base instincts," "psychologically defective" beings, and "violent" criminals. Alongside representations such as these, one discovers that those who find themselves ensnared in the criminal justice system are not unlikely to receive relatively severe penalties. While the fines imposed for graffiti are on the increase, there is growing pressure on judges and other relevant authorities to sentence writers to prison. Although not yet a routine punishment, the fact that prison sentences are being imposed suggests that negative, emotively charged portrayals of graffiti writing are normalizing extremely punitive reactions.

Insofar as the empirical evidence that might justify such strong condemnations of graffiti is absent, it is also reasonable to conclude that the criterion of disproportionality is satisfied. Moreover, disproportionately is demonstrated by the willingness of officials to hunt down legal forms of graffiti. This is especially evident as they go about publicly condemning "graffiti sympathizers" and the *aesthetics* of graffiti. State actors have gone so far as to call on the law, or mobilize their access to the criminal justice system, for the sake of banishing legal and cultural appropriations of the "graffiti look." Most ironically perhaps, in crafting legislation that seeks to undermine the aesthetic rights to private property, the city has demonstrated its willingness to engage in the very practices for which it routinely condemns graffiti writers.

CHAPTER 6

# Engendering Desire for Neoliberal Penality and the Logic of Growth Machines

**Abstract** Previous accounts have interpreted opposition to graffiti as a way to normalize state authority and deflect attention away from crises in capitalism. This chapter appreciates the need to connect antigraffiti rhetoric to broader structural forces, but posits that it is more likely a product of neoliberal statecrafting and the desire to commodify space. Neoliberal states are marked by an increased reliance on coercive mechanisms to control the social tensions that accompany growing inequality. Led by landed capitalists, the commodification of space entails enticing corporations to the city, gentrifying neighborhoods, and turning the city into a middle-class tourist destination. Opposition to graffiti provides one mechanism to articulate and normalize these objectives, even though they do not necessarily serve the interests of city residents.

**Keywords** Neoliberalism · Punishment · Urban · Growth machines · Privatism · Technology · Fetish

Although there may be agreement on how to recognize a panic when it occurs, there is less agreement on what motivates powerful social groups to overreact to relatively inconsequential behaviors. According to Erikson,[1] for

---

[1] Erikson, *Wayward Puritans* (1966).

example, the need to maintain social solidarity drives panics, but for Hall and colleagues[2] they are governed by the need to divert attention away from crises of capitalism. In constructing a typology of panics, Goode and Ben-Yehuda[3] argue that various social groups, for a wide array of reasons, may craft them.

Two previous studies have assumed that the moral panic concept could be meaningfully applied in analyzing responses to graffiti writing. The first, Ferrell's study of graffiti writing in Denver, Colorado, argued that city opposition to the practice was grounded in the need to reinforce public acceptance of the state's ability to exercise authority over its subjects.[4] The second was conducted by Austin and, based on graffiti writing in New York City throughout the 1970s and the 1980s, argued that official opposition to graffiti worked to deflect attention away from capitalism during a period of crisis.[5] Following Ferrell and Austin, it is important to recognize that the state and economic trends are central to comprehending responses to graffiti.

However, this chapter suggests that moral panics over graffiti are better understood when situated against two structural dynamics associated with "late capitalist" societies: neoliberal state-crafting and, closely related, the commodification of urban space. The hallmarks of neoliberalism include growing economic inequalities and larger portions of the population having a tenuous connection to labor markets. In the USA and other regions adopting neoliberal models of social life, the state responds to those who are more or less excluded from the economy in extremely punitive ways.[6] In light of such trends, I argue that graffiti operates as a "gateway penality." That is, it provides an easy target that political elites can readily disparage and, in the course of doing so, normalize the punitive responses to the social problems that accompany neoliberal governance.

At the urban level, antigraffiti rhetoric and practice serves the interests of what Logan and Molotch refer to as the "growth machine"[7] or, more

---

[2] Hall et al., *Policing the* Crisis (1978).
[3] Goode and Ben-Yehuda, *Moral Panics* (1994).
[4] Ferrell, *Crimes of Style* (1993).
[5] Austin, *Taking the Train* (2001).
[6] Wacquant, *Punishing the Poor* (2009b); Pratt and Eriksson, *Contrasts in Punishment* (2013).
[7] Logan and Molotch, *Urban Fortunes* (1987).

simply put, landed capital. Growth machines ultimately seek to extract the maximum profit possible from how space is put to use, and do so at the expense of those who use land for the satisfaction of basic, fundamental needs. Particular strategies of urban growth include enticing corporations to locate their headquarters in the city, gentrifying neighborhoods, and transforming the environment into a hospitable tourist destination for privileged social classes. As their discourse makes clear, political elites perceive graffiti as a threat to such interests and something that must therefore be eradicated from the city.

## COMPETING THEORIES ON MORAL PANICS

In what is arguably one of the most important works on the topic, Goode and Ben-Yehuda[8] identify three distinct theories that account for moral panics: a "grassroots," an "interest group," and an "elite-engineered" model. The grassroots model argues that "panics originate with the general public" and are motivated by genuine moral concerns.[9] In this view, the elite and other interest groups cannot conjure panics out of thin air as their needs may dictate. Rather, privileged social groups can only respond to latent concerns that are prevalent among the general public.

The interest group model asserts that specific groups, such as professional associations, police departments, and the mass media, have independent reasons for drawing public attention toward certain issues. In such cases, it is often difficult to draw a hard line between ideological and material interests. For example, police officials may sincerely believe that crime needs to be reduced, and this belief may entail the allocation of greater resources to police departments.[10]

According to the third model identified by Goode and Ben-Yehuda—elite engineering—powerful elites "deliberately and consciously" create panics over problems that contain little, if any, objective threat to the public. As there is no objective threat, it follows that panics are engineered to distract the public from problems the solution of which would

---

[8] Goode and Ben-Yehuda, *Moral Panics*, 124–127.
[9] Ibid., 127.
[10] Ibid., 139.

"threaten or undermine the interests of the elite."[11] Economically powerful social groups usually succeed in the practical and ideological implementation of their ideas because of their overaccess to the media and ability to drive the legislative process. It almost goes without saying that the interests of the elite are contrary, if not antagonistic to, the interests of the general public.[12]

While this delineation of models is noteworthy for its conciseness, its limitations emerge when Erikson's *Wayward Puritans*[13] is categorized as an example of the grassroots model[14] and the work of Hall and colleagues[15] is used to illustrate the elite-engineered model.[16] The problem is not so much that this approach misrepresents the work of Erikson and Hall and others, but that it does not adequately capture the ways in which such theorists emphasize the broader social "functions" fulfilled by moral panics.

Grounded in Durkheim's[17] ideas concerning the "collective conscious," Erikson[18] claims that deviance is a major resource for maintaining the moral boundaries of a society. This is because deviance and deviant acts are likely to generate "publicity, a moment of excitement and alarm, a feeling that something needs to be done."[19] In other words, deviance provides the raw material that sustains moral panics. Erikson encourages us to perceive panics as a mechanism to reinforce those norms and values that come to be seen as legitimate by the members of a society and, as such, perceived to ensure social harmony. Importantly, this process transpires independently of the conscious intentions of the actors involved, such as "rule enforcers," "deviants," and the "audience." In this sense, we can say that the reproduction of communal solidarity takes place "behind the backs" of the actors involved and the community.

[11] Ibid., 135.
[12] Ibid., 138.
[13] Erikson, *Wayward Puritans* (1966).
[14] Goode and Ben-Yehuda, *Moral Panics*, 128.
[15] Hall et al., *Policing the Crisis* (1978).
[16] Goode and Ben-Yehuda, *Moral Panics*, 135–138.
[17] Durkheim, *Division of Labor* (1960).
[18] Erikson, *Wayward Puritans*, 4, 196.
[19] Ibid., 69.

Aspects of the puritan settlement in seventeenth-century Massachusetts serve as the empirical basis for Erikson's broader theoretical claims. On the one hand, he shows that deviants were often identified and brought to trial by authorities despite the fact that the latter had difficulty specifying exactly which legal thresholds deviants had transgressed.[20] From a legal perspective, the trials are clearly absurd, yet, as Erikson points out, "when the whole affair is seen as a ceremony and not as a test of guilt, as a demonstration rather than an inquiry, its accents and rhythms are easier to understand."[21] On the other hand, and following the notion that deviance is "functional" for a society, Erikson shows how the deviancy rate within the puritan settlements remained relatively stable over time.[22] This suggests that deviance is not so much a problem to be solved, but a *resource* that needs to be *maintained, regulated*, and *deployed* as necessary.

Following the likes of Marx and Gramsci, Hall and colleagues argue that capitalist societies are conflictual, not consensual, in nature. The fundamental conflict occurs between capital and labor and pertains to the material conditions in which capitalists exploit labor power for profit. Capitalists rely on two methods to prevent the emergence of open class conflict. The first, hegemony, suggests that through ideological means capitalists win the consent of the laboring classes to an economic structure that is exploitative. The second involves deploying the state's monopoly on the legitimate use of violence to control the working classes. When crises in the mode of production occur, already tense social relations are stretched to breaking point and consent is lost. During such moments, we are likely to see open class conflict, which will compel the state to use force in order to preserve capital. Yet the state must also win consent to such uses of force.[23]

It is within this broader context that Hall and colleagues come to see panics as ideological maneuvers that emerge for the purpose of winning consent to the use of force, which is deployed for the sake of preserving capitalism in times of crisis. Moral panics, in this view, suppress the contradiction between capital

---

[20] Ibid., 93.
[21] Ibid., 103.
[22] Ibid., 171–181.
[23] Hall et al., *Policing the Crisis* (1978).

and labor by suggesting that the fundamental relations of society are not those between two very unequal classes, but those between the civil and the uncivil; the law-abiding and the criminal. Working-class consent is won by propagating the notion that the state guards against a Hobbesian "state of nature" rather than, as Marxists would argue, ensure the smooth functioning of an economic system in which capital exploits labor.[24]

While accepting that the contradiction between capital and labor is important, scholars such as Watney[25] and Thompson[26] suggest that it is only one conflict within a broad range of struggles. Rather than pacify class antagonisms, panics seek to regulate and discipline bodies such that predictable forms of collective behavior are engendered. They work by propagating discourses that distinguish "normal" behavior (and therefore "acceptable") from "abnormal" behavior (and therefore "unacceptable"). For the most part, the authority and legitimacy that moral panics muster is a function of their originating from within institutionalized fields of knowledge, such as the "human sciences," or of their repetition in the mass media.

In this light, moral panics are not volatile ruptures in public discourse, but moments in:

> The mobility of ideological confrontation across the entire field of public representations, and in particular those handling and evaluating the meanings of the human body, where rival and incompatible forces and values are involved in a ceaseless struggle to define supposedly universal "human" truths.[27]

This suggests that the regulatory ends toward which moral panics may be directed are more diverse than Erikson and Hall and colleagues would lead us to believe. Indeed, whereas Watney goes on to interpret the moral panic over AIDS as a conservative effort to police sexuality such that the ideal of the heterosexual nuclear family is defended,[28] Thompson has shown a connection between a variety of panics and the development of new forms

---

[24] Chambliss and Mankoff, *Whose Law?* 15–16 (1976).
[25] Watney, *Policing Desire* (1987).
[26] Thompson, *Moral Panics* (1998).
[27] Watney, *Policing Desire*, 42.
[28] Ibid., 43, 146.

of bodily regulation in a post–World War II era marked by major structural, technological, and cultural changes.[29]

It would be pointless to deny that these major approaches to panics can help us understand certain aspects of New York City's reaction to graffiti. For example, whereas Erikson makes it possible to question what would otherwise appear to be a transparent response to graffiti writing culture, accounts that emphasize competing interests suggest that the reproduction of power relations is somehow at stake. However, rather than adjudicate between these models, my goal will be to highlight the importance of other structural dimensions that, although overlooked thus far, seem central to accounting for contemporary panics over graffiti. More specifically, I want to link New York City's panic over graffiti writing to neoliberal state-crafting and urban commodification.

## The Punitive Tendencies Inherent to Neoliberalism: Graffiti as a "Gateway" to Harsh Punishment

Much recent scholarship characterizes the latter part of the twentieth century as one marked by the rise and subsequent entrenchment of neoliberalism. According to Wacquant,[30] neoliberalism can be understood as a new state formation that relentlessly extends the commodification process and controls the social body through draconian public policy and prisons. The outcomes of neoliberalism include extreme social inequalities, high rates of underemployment, and the withdrawal of robust social support programs. The social insecurity that neoliberalism forces individuals to endure is glossed over through ideologies of personal responsibility.

As this conceptualization intimates, the neoliberal state has overwhelmingly embraced punitive responses to deviance and those who find themselves excluded from the labor market, marking a significant retreat from the idea that it has an obligation to address poverty and inequality through public assistance. This is often rationalized by claiming that it is individuals who are responsible for maintaining continuous employment

---

[29] Thompson, *Moral Panics*, 139–142.
[30] Wacquant, *Prisons of Poverty* (2009a); Wacquant, "Crafting the Neoliberal State" (2010).

and avoiding poverty, and by a culture that valorizes political elites who promise to be "tough on crime."[31]

The punitive turn inherent to neoliberal state-crafting does not come cheap. While its advocates often claim that neoliberalism is efficient due to pushing for "small governments," the costs of expansive penal policy are massive. To give but a few examples from the literature, Wacquant points out that between 1980 and 1997, the USA increased its criminal justice budget by $100 billion, that police budgets grew fourfold, and funding for incarceration grew sixfold.[32] The significance of the resources poured into the state's punitive branches becomes especially salient when juxtaposed with other budgets. To draw from Wacquant once again, by 1995 the USA was "spending twice as much to incarcerate ($46 billion) as to support destitute single mothers with children ($20 billion), and as much as AFDC and food stamps put together."[33] Furthermore, neoliberal states routinely withdraw resources from areas such as education and health care to bolster the criminal justice sector. According to Shelden and Brown,[34] toward the end of the late 1980s the number of employees in California's prison system had grown by 169 % while higher education saw a decrease of 8.7 % in its workforce. Moreover, by 1996 "the average annual salary of a guard stood at $44,000—a figure that is 58 % above the national average" and "more than $10,000 above teachers."

The 1980s and the 1990s were pivotal moments in the rapid expansion of criminal justice, but the type of overspending seen in this domain has by no means abated. It is embarrassing to admit, but to allay concerns that criminology majors have around their future employability, I often reference the "robust" nature of state expenditures on criminal justice, assuring them that it remains the one area where a secure job with the state is a real possibility.

Although the public effectively funds this expensive system, it is not one that generates much by way of overall social benefit. It is routinely accepted among critical scholars that the nature of contemporary labor markets, combined with things like the quest for profit that governs

---

[31] Pratt and Eriksson, *Contrasts in Punishment* (2013).
[32] Wacquant, *Prisons of Poverty*, 68.
[33] Ibid.
[34] Shelden and Brown, "Crime Control Industry," 45 (2000).

privatized prisons, renders the idea of socially reintegrating prisoners in any meaningful sense moot.[35] In neoliberal times, attempting to rehabilitate prisoners through education or work training are costs that can simply be eliminated, not to mention that there is not much of a labor market to return to in any case.

All of which raises a dilemma: How to entice the public to desire the neoliberal order? How to "win consent" to an organization of social life that does not serve the best interests of the vast majority of society? Considered in this light, it is not hard to see graffiti writing subculture as replete with attributes that make it an ideal candidate to exploit for the sake of legitimizing neoliberalism, especially its punitive tendencies. The activities that graffiti writers engage in appear to be governed by the pursuit of pleasure and enjoyment, thereby embodying a rejection of the protestant work ethic and the sense of responsibility that this often implies. At the same time, graffiti writers do not have ready access to communication channels that could be used to explain their behavior, and their practices transpire within a long discursive and material history that denounces graffiti. In these ways, they are profoundly powerless. As an inherently public act, the broader community is often compelled to encounter the best and worst works of graffiti, which can foster resentment among middle classes and property owners. Given the energy expended on encouraging the view that graffiti writing is an inherently problematic practice, such resentment is almost a fait accompli.

Bearing this in mind, it is no accident that graffiti is a frequent theme within political discourse and can be understood as what I would refer to as a "gateway penality." An obvious play on the idea of "gateway drugs," a phrase that is most interesting for its persuasive aura, gateway penality suggests that the state must work its way toward widespread acceptance of its desire to relentlessly punish. Subcultures that revolve around behaviors that seem nonutilitarian, or lacking any economic necessity, whose participants are socially marginalized and therefore easily stigmatized, are difficult to portray with sympathy. Situated as such, they become sites

---

[35] The idea of prison and reform being mutually exclusive is a recurrent thread in critical literature on punishment. See, for example, Rusche and Kirchheimer, *Punishment and Social Structure* (1939/1968); Feeley and Simon, "New Penology" (1992); Kramer, Rajah, and Sung, "Neoliberal Prisons" (2013); Rajah, Kramer, and Sung, "Changing Narrative Accounts" (2014).

where the extremely punitive logic required to regulate the social problems that accompany exclusionary social orders can be articulated and exercised with relative impunity. Once such measures become normalized and routine, they can extend to other "objectionable" behaviors as they emerge.

Although certainly not the only example, graffiti writing is also an arena in which the irrational costs of punitive social policy can be portrayed as natural and inevitable, as if there were simply no alternative to exorbitant spending on behaviors and practices that "offend" the neoliberal order for one reason or another. This is particularly evident in mass media stories and political press releases that inform the public of the latest technological developments in the war on graffiti.[36]

The *New York Times* once reported that a company known for the construction of lasers capable of shooting down missiles and igniting miniature hydrogen bombs had decided to veer away from its usual adventures in the military sphere and take a shot at tackling the graffiti problem. The company developed an antigraffiti weapon that, described with a degree of enthusiasm that almost sounds fetishistic, relies on a "100-watt green beam, pulsing up to 1,000 times a second."[37] When the beam strikes a surface covered with graffiti, the "beam's energy is converted into sound waves," which hit the underlying surface. They then rebound to cause a miniature explosion that "pulverizes and removes the paint as a fine dust." Irrespective of its sophistication, the device comes with a price tag that renders it unfit for inclusion in the "urban warfare" market: even if produced in quantity, the antigraffiti laser beam would "cost about $250,000."[38]

While devices such as this may be too expensive to exist as anything other than fantastic objects of desire, those in political authority have sought to fulfill their visions of a graffiti-free city in other ways. A middle ground seems to have been found in "state-of-the-art" graffiti removal trucks.[39] Developed by the Department of Sanitation toward the late

---

[36] Much of the material presented in preceding chapters also supports this contention.
[37] Browne, "Laser Weapon," Section 1, 36 (1996).
[38] Ibid.
[39] Louie, "Graffitibusters!" Section F, 3 (1998).

1990s, such trucks typically include an electronic sensor capable of determining the color of a wall beneath layers of graffiti. Having determined this color, a computer and paint mixer are then used to produce that color on the spot. This color-matching equipment is complemented by a paint sprayer and, for those cases in which repainting is inappropriate, a power washer is also included.

The effectiveness of the "wundertruck" may be measured according to how many square feet of graffiti it can remove per day: whereas "traditional" methods of graffiti concealment "cover less than 2000 square feet of graffiti per day with no guaranteed color match,"[40] the antigraffiti truck is capable of getting "rid of more than 20,000 square feet per day."[41] There were at least 10 such trucks "patrolling" the boroughs of New York City by the early 2000s.[42] Now seen as indispensable to the urban "war" on graffiti, each of these "tanks" cost somewhere in the vicinity of $130,000.[43]

In relation to policing graffiti, this has been entrusted to the Anti-Graffiti Task Force,[44] which initially emerged during the 1970s under the Lindsay administration. At this stage, it was an informal agency that consisted of eight city agencies.[45] Some 20 years later, on July 11, 1995, Giuliani signed an executive order that transformed the Anti-Graffiti Task Force into an official city agency. Upon becoming a permanent fixture of the city's formal bureaucracy, it included 16 city agencies.[46] Within a year or so, it would seem that four more agencies were added to the Task Force.[47] Furthermore, within the NYPD—obviously one of the central

---

[40] Bruce Pienkny, owner of Graffiti Answers, quoted in Engels, "Graffiti-Cleaning Crew," Suburban, 2 (2001).
[41] Ibid.
[42] Perez, "Brush-Off to Graffiti," Suburban, 1.
[43] Ibid.
[44] The Task Force unites city agencies that are in any way connected to the "graffiti problem" or its resolution.
[45] See the earlier chapter on graffiti in the 1970s and the 1980s.
[46] Giuliani Files, "Executive Order No. 24," (1995c).
[47] Giuliani Files, "Anti-Graffiti Expo' 96" (1996). Document found in the folder listed above. This document lists representatives from 20 city agencies as members of the task force.

agencies of the Task Force—the number of police officers assigned to antigraffiti work has increased in recent years. As 1994 drew to a close, the NYPD's Anti-Graffiti Squad consisted of 25 officers.[48] By early 2005, this squad had more than tripled to include 76 officers.[49]

There are several aspects to the frequent reporting on technological developments in the war on graffiti that make it quite remarkable. As intimated, it tends to fetishize technological advancements, often construing each latest gadget as *the* solution to the graffiti problem. Technologies premised upon control rarely fail to figure as repositories of faith, potent signifiers that allow individuals to feel optimistic about a better, safer, future. While the costs of new technologies and the extent of resources devoted to antigraffiti are consistently emphasized, rarely is the wisdom of such expenditure questioned. Rather, it is simply assumed that such financial burdens are inevitable.

Not surprisingly perhaps, such discourses tend to ignore the possibility that the faith in technological, repressive solutions might be misplaced. This occurs even though it is readily apparent that it is ineffective. The Anti-Graffiti Task Force, for example, rapidly grows from a handful of agencies to 20, from 25 to 76 officers, and becomes a permanent city office, yet the peculiarity of all this remains unquestioned.

Concerning graffiti removal efforts, the city generally assesses its progress by charting the volume of square feet removed per year. In 1998, Giuliani announced that since 1994 the Department of Transportation alone had removed approximately 24 million square feet of graffiti from the city.[50] Based on available documents, I would estimate that from 1994 to 1998 the city[51] removed approximately 60 million square feet of graffiti, or 12–15 million square feet per year.[52] While this may sound impressive, its impact on eradicating graffiti is questionable. Even with

---

[48] Onishi, "All He Wrote," Section 13, 10; Seifman, "Rudy Will Ed-ucate," 20 (1994).

[49] Bloomberg Files, "Re-Launch 'Operation Impact'" (2005a); Sclafani, "Spray It Ain't So," Suburban, 46 (2005b). This article claims that the Citywide Vandals Task Force consists of 80 police officers.

[50] Giuliani Files, "Giuliani Continues Assault" (1998).

[51] That is, all the city agencies that remove graffiti combined.

[52] Giuliani Files, Folder Title: "Police Department – Graffiti" (1996). Location: Folder # 0141; Roll # 60696 (NYC Municipal Archives).

persistent efforts throughout the intervening years, in 2005 Bloomberg announced that the city had removed approximately 57 million square feet of graffiti in the two preceding years,[53] or 28.5 million square feet per year. Although it is difficult to say anything conclusive about the rate of graffiti based on these figures, they do seem to suggest that graffiti is a relatively persistent feature of New York City's urban landscape.

Insofar as exact figures are hard to come by, assessing the cost of all this removal is quite a gray area. However, it would seem that New York City spends approximately $5–10 million a year on graffiti removal. Incidentally, many cities throughout the world seem to claim that antigraffiti efforts cost somewhere in the vicinity of $5 million per year. One might suspect that this has somehow become a magical figure, one that arouses public animosity toward graffiti but does not go so far as to raise questions concerning the logic of spending such an amount on graffiti removal.

Increases in the amount of graffiti being removed and in the number of city agencies and police officers assigned to antigraffiti work suggest that the city's efforts—when measured in terms of keeping graffiti out of the public square and deterring graffiti writers—are not being met with much success. If such efforts were successful, one would expect to see steady *decreases* in the amount of resources necessary for antigraffiti initiatives.

It is important to recall that much of the concern with eradicating graffiti is based on the assumption that this will decrease serious crime. Another way to put this would be to say that it is the threat of serious crime that legitimates the attention directed toward petty crimes. But, if this is so, why not utilize resources to focus directly on serious crime? After all, research shows that this is a more effective method.[54]

Further, in emphasizing things like surveillance, control, and suppression, the chance for a dialogue occurring between those in authority and New York City's graffiti writers seems to fall further and further from view. In light of the fact that graffiti writers of today are capable of producing aesthetically pleasing works of public art, this closing off of a dialogue is quite peculiar. Moreover, it would seem that many graffiti writers, provided they are given artistic freedom, are not opposed to producing such

---

[53] Bloomberg Files, "Re-Launch 'Operation Impact'" (2005a).
[54] See the academic critiques of broken windows offered in the previous chapter.

works free of charge. And, as has been noted, the public does not appear to dislike elaborate forms of graffiti.[55] Yet, instead of encouraging an urban art form that the public appreciates, and which could conceivably save the city from some relatively large monetary expenditure, New York City's public officials adamantly refuse to build working relationships with graffiti writers.

All this would seem to indicate that the city's antigraffiti efforts are not only "unsuccessful," but are somewhat mysterious. To put it somewhat poignantly, why devote substantial resources and energy, presumably at the expense of more pressing concerns, to ensure city walls are noteworthy for not much more than uniform veneers of "Mission Brown" and "Tioga Grey"? Consistent with Erikson's skepticism, the antigraffiti performances orchestrated by city officials convey meanings and ideas that go well beyond their surface level. The problem is not so much one of graffiti removal, but one of *exploiting* graffiti for the sake of normalizing the logic of neoliberal state-crafting.

## MORAL PANICS AND URBAN DYNAMICS: THE GROWTH MACHINE AND PRIVATISM

The political response to graffiti is further fueled by growth machines operating at the urban level. According to Logan and Molotch,[56] growth machines are loose coalitions that form between local political elites, landowners, corporate developers, and speculators (i.e., landed capitalists). These actors are united by their shared interest in extracting the maximum profit possible from how land is put to use and invariably operate without much concern for ensuring that land is used in ways that serve the greater social good. To put it in Marxist terminology, growth machines focus on cities as sites of "exchange value" rather than "use value."

---

[55] It might also be worth noting that contrary to what political elites often claim, indirect evidence suggests that the public are not overly concerned with graffiti. For example, the ratio of noise to graffiti complaints as indicated by calls to 311 is 100 to 1. For noise complaints, see Bloomberg Files, "'Operation Silent Night'" (2002a); Bloomberg Files, "Our Quality of Life" (2002b). For the "100 to 1" ratio referred to see Editorial, "Shoot Down," 24 (1997); See also Colangelo, "Noise Bill," 18 (2005).

[56] Logan and Molotch, *Urban Fortunes* (1987).

The ideology of privatism ensures the smooth functioning of the growth machine. Privatism asserts that if the public sector facilitates the accumulation of private capital by offering businesses tax incentives and providing them with necessary infrastructure, a better economic climate will be created. This climate is good because it invites businesses to the city, which creates jobs and increases the tax base. A greater pool of wealth signifies material gains that will inevitably "trickle down" such that all of the city's residents stand to benefit. To put this as succinctly as possible, privatism could easily be understood as an interpretation of urban environments that is heavily indebted to some core principles of neoliberalism (states should facilitate the accumulation of private capital, privatized wealth is a social good, etc.).[57]

The most important—and most obvious—feature of privatism is its evocation of what one might be inclined to call a causal logic. Insofar as this is the case, public–private partnerships can be considered an independent variable, whereas the presence of stable business communities and better living conditions for city residents figure as dependent variables. Mirroring privatism, antigraffiti rhetoric claims that business communities and living conditions are dependent variables. Instead of emphasizing public–private partnerships, however, antigraffiti rhetoric claims that business and "quality of life" are adversely affected by the *presence* of graffiti:

[Graffiti] hurts business because it turns the street into a frightening place.[58]
The graffiti affects everyone's quality of life. It's ugly and it brings down property values.[59]
Graffiti poses a direct threat to the quality of life of all New Yorkers.[60]

Officials also articulate the flipside to this logic, often claiming that stable business communities and environments that are beneficial for all city residents are generated in the *absence* of graffiti:

---

[57] For further detail concerning "privatism," see Logan and Molotch, *Urban Fortunes* (1987); Squires, "Partnership" (2011).
[58] Probation Commissioner Raul Russi quoted in Bertrand, "Graffiti Vandals Unpainting," Suburban, 1 (1997).
[59] Coordinator of the 106th precinct Sal Petrozzino quoted in Lemire, "Graffiti Kids," Suburban, 1 (2002a).
[60] Bloomberg quoted in Saul, "Mike Vows," Suburban, 1.

Last July, we launched a citywide campaign to cleanup graffiti... Not only does that keep New Yorkers safe; it also helps sustain neighborhoods where people want to live and businesses want to locate and invest.[61]

[G]raffiti hurts neighborhoods both aesthetically and economically. To boost New York City's economy and create jobs, it's critical to create neighborhoods where people want to live and businesses want to locate and invest.[62]

Not only are we cleaning graffiti, we also send a message to people around the city that our neighborhood is a great place to live and raise a family.[63]

These [anti-graffiti] initiatives not only improve the quality of life for New Yorkers, but show visitors that New York is a clean, responsible, vibrant city.[64]

The elective affinity between antigraffiti rhetoric and the ideology of privatism is transparent to the point where it hardly calls for further comment. It is, however, worth noting that statements such as these are far from difficult to find. If anything, they are repeated to such an extent that it would not be unfair to say that antigraffiti discourse is constituted by a handful of major "sound bites." Coterminous with this repetition, the opposition to graffiti is expressed in syntactic structures noteworthy for their simplicity, declarative tone, and almost perfect lucidity.

Decoding antigraffiti rhetoric as a variation of privatism, thereby exposing its ideological bearings, suggests that we are not in the presence of free-floating discourses, but the "growth machine." That political elites have certainly come to perceive graffiti as something that interferes with the kinds of objectives established by growth machines is neatly encapsulated in the following passage:

Graffiti adversely affects the city's economy by reducing property values and discouraging tourism... The consequences of graffiti include businesses relocating to other cities or states and tourists foregoing trips to New York City.[65]

[61] Bloomberg Files, "Making Our City" (2003e).
[62] Economic Development Corporation president Andrew Alper quoted in Bloomberg Files, "Bloomberg Updates Citywide Graffiti" (2003d).
[63] City Council member Eric Gioia quoted in Yaniv, "Spray and Wash," Suburban, 2 (2005).
[64] Giuliani Files, "Giuliani Removes Graffiti" (1995b).
[65] Giuliani Files, "Anti-Graffiti Expo '96" (1996).

This statement has the additional virtue of illuminating the ideal city as conceptualized by political elites. In their worldview, the best of all possible cities is one that successfully promotes tourism, ensures high property values, and caters to the needs of business.[66] Consistent with what the notion of privatism would lead us to expect, these objectives are often legitimated by claiming that their pursuit will serve the interests of all city residents.[67] Unfortunately, however, the critical research in this area does not verify the notion that general benefit follows from the obsession with "economic development," "boosting" the city's reputation, and so on.

Scholars have shown how the desire to turn a city into a middle-class tourist destination often entails the "disneyfication" of urban spaces, or what others have referred to as "themed environments," which reinforces reified social relations and invites aggressive competition between spatial regions.[68] Moreover, critical scholars have found that the tourism industry, as one of the major pillars in a "postindustrial" economy, is dependent

---

[66] By no means should it be thought that the statement just presented stands in isolation. Rather, its basic message is conveyed with some degree of regularity: "Litter, dirt, vandalism, and graffiti destroy the beauty of our City, discourage business and tourism" [Giuliani Files, "Proclamation to We Care" (1995d)]. And, "*Good criminal justice policy is good economic development policy.* We are ... making the community more hospitable for investment" [Criminal Justice Coordinator John Feinblatt quoted in Bloomberg Files, "Queens Plaza Clean-up" (2003b); emphasis added].

[67] Giuliani Files, "Adopt-A-Highway" (1995a); Giuliani Files, "Proclamation to We Care" (1995d); Giuliani Files, "Staten Island, Gramercy Park" (1995e); Bloomberg Files, "Bloomberg Delivers 2003" (2003a); Bloomberg Files, "Driving Crime Down" (2003c).

[68] On these points see Sorkin, *Variations on a Theme Park* (1992); Eco, *Travels* (1986); Gottdiener, *Theming of America*, 86–88; Sassen, *Global City* (2001); Urry, *Tourist Gaze* (1990). Bloomberg clearly embraces this competitive spirit between cities and, more importantly, the way in which this stance readily accepts that the city is best understood and treated as a commodity: "New York is in a fierce, worldwide competition; our strategy must be to hone our competitive advantages. We must offer the best product—and sell it, forcefully." Also, "To oversee our promotion and marketing efforts, we'll establish a chief Marketing Officer for the city ... we'll take advantage of our brand" [Bloomberg Files, "Bloomberg Delivers 2003" (2003a)].

upon low-paying jobs that, along with demanding a psychologically taxing form of "emotional labor" from employees, offer very few benefits or opportunities for career advancement.[69]

In relation to property values, it is important to note the way in which public officials tend to assume that the value of property is somehow absolute; as if it existed somewhere beyond social, economic, and political contexts. This assumption is embedded, for example, in Giuliani's assertion that "graffiti reduces property values."[70] In this view, property values are construed as given a priori and, as graffiti appears, this value decreases. However, the value of property is an overdetermined phenomenon that tends to fluctuate in relation to broader economic and political circumstances.[71] More importantly, urban sociologists have argued that as property values increase not everyone stands to benefit. For those who are homeless, but also for those who do not own property and are therefore compelled to pay rent,[72] rising property values imply higher costs of basic living. As is well documented by research on gentrification and the use of business improvement districts (BIDs) to "clean-up" public space, this can often lead to the displacement of socially marginalized and working-class populations.[73]

Pushing this line of analysis further, Neil Smith[74] and Mike Davis[75] suggest that as overdevelopment generates areas of concentrated privilege, the need to defend such enclaves inevitably follows. This often

---

[69] Sherman, *Class Acts* (2007). For a prescient critique of the service industry, see Braverman, *Labor and Monopoly Capital* (1974); see also Wilson, *Truly Disadvantaged* (1987).

[70] Giuliani Files, "Anti-Graffiti Expo '96" (1996).

[71] Smith, *New Urban Frontier* (1996).

[72] Most people in New York City do not own property. According to the 2000 census, only 30.2 % of New York City's population owns their own home, which is about half the national average.

[73] Zukin, *Landscapes of Power* (1991); Massey and Denton, *American Apartheid* (1993). On Business Improvement Districts, see Mitchell, *Right to the City* (2003); Sites, *Remaking New York* (2003); Stokes, "Business Improvement Districts" (2006); Walsh, "Union Square Park" (2006); Ward, "'Policies in Motion'" (2006).

[74] Smith, *New Urban Frontier* (1996).

[75] Davis, *City of Quartz* (1990); Davis, *Dead Cities* (2002).

translates into an overpolicing of certain neighborhoods, the militarization of public space, and draconian uses of the law. In other words, public officials routinely rely upon agencies of social control and their monopoly over the use of force to address the growth machine's limitations.

Those who do stand to benefit from rising property values are, of course, those who are in a position to buy property. Although this group consists of individuals from the middle and upper classes, it is generally constituted by land developers and those who purchase property as a speculative investment.[76] Renters and other socially marginalized groups rarely derive any advantages from the wealth these entities generate for themselves.

Finally, not all New Yorkers stand to benefit when the city caters to the needs of business. In conjunction with tax incentives, enticing businesses to the city—especially "big business"—usually means spending public monies on the infrastructure that they require. The political elite often justify this kind of "public–private" partnership by claiming that the public will see large returns on their investment:

> When we lead with public infrastructure...the private market will follow. *The investment will be substantial—but the value created will be far greater.* Here...the public sector can pay for improvements—with revenues generated by future economic activity.[77]

While the public's "substantial investment" may entice the private sector and may generate wealth, it is worth drawing attention toward what is often

---

[76] Logan and Molotch, *Urban Fortunes* (1987).
[77] Bloomberg Files, "Bloomberg Delivers 2003" (2003a). It is worth noting that there are many moments in the political discourse under scrutiny where the importance of being business-friendly is emphasized. The following examples are illustrative: "We're also getting our economy back on track by making New York a more attractive place for major corporate employers" [Bloomberg Files, "Neighborhood by Neighborhood" (2003e)]; "We're making New York business-friendly. That means creating the infrastructure needed for economic growth [Bloomberg Files, "State of the City" (2004a)]; "We're going to invest in economic development projects, make New York the most business-friendly city in the nation..." [Bloomberg Files, "2006 State of the City" (2006)].

omitted from such statements: namely, any mention of the policies or strategies that will ensure promised financial gains flow back into the public sector. Instead, political leaders tend to assume that "private interests" will self-regulate and that this will guarantee an equitable redistribution of monetary gains. That this perspective is mysteriously silent when it comes to questions of redistribution is no accident. As urban sociologists have shown, not only do material gains often fail to transpire, but efforts at "growth" often exacerbate urban dilemmas, such as class inequality, racial segregation, and social and environmental problems.[78]

That city-level political administrations often allow the private sector to more or less determine how urban spaces will be put to use is no secret. In accordance with the critical analyses of urban sociologists, however, it becomes very difficult to accept the notion that the arrangement between growth machines and the state works to the benefit of "all New Yorkers" when Bloomberg, with exuberance, says:

> Residential property values have appreciated by more than 80% over the last four years.[79]

And,

> [T]he percentage of [misdemeanor] defendants receiving jail sentences has increased 48%, with sentences of more than 30 days increasing 74%.[80]

Within less than a year of this communiqué, which celebrates growth in the incarceration rate, the progress being made concerning higher rates of imprisonment was once again noted:

> [T]he percentage of cases resulting in jail time has increased from 45% to 67%.[81]

This would seem to suggest that not all New Yorkers benefit when growth machines dominate the decision-making process that ultimately determines how urban land will be utilized. As growth machines recreate the urban environment, from which some do stand to gain, many are

---

[78] Logan and Molotch, *Urban* Fortunes, 85–98; Squires, "Partnership" (2011).
[79] Bloomberg Files, "Crime Reduction Strategies" (2005b).
[80] Bloomberg Files, "Historic Crime Reduction" (2004b).
[81] Bloomberg Files, "Crime Reduction Strategies" (2005b).

displaced or, even worse, become entangled with the city's carceral complex. For anybody who is familiar with New York City, or has witnessed the changing social composition of urban neighborhoods in areas of the USA subjected to the gentrification process, the way in which space can be rapidly created anew will seem fairly obvious.

The mechanisms that make such changes possible are, however, slightly less obvious. There is little to support the view that a strong relationship between graffiti and "disorder," or the economic and social vitality of a city, exists. For a theory that outlines how the fundamental social and economic contours of a city are profoundly shaped by growth machines, which seek public approval and legitimacy through ideological means, according importance to visual factors within the urban environment is nonsensical.

Understood in this context, the antigraffiti rhetoric and initiatives orchestrated by public officials in New York City can be read as a variation on the ideology of privatism,[82] which ultimately serve the interests of growth machines. However, insofar as antigraffiti rhetoric links efforts at crime reduction to the economic and social order of things, it offers a much more palatable version of privatism. The rhetorical tropes embedded within antigraffiti discourse are incredibly effective because they operate on the premise, by and largely correct, that it is a risk to assume that people will readily accept the idea that general benefits follow from the public subsidization of "big business." Conceivably, however, people are more likely to support anticrime initiatives.

It is important to note that none of this amounts to the claim that the consciousness of the masses is somehow "false" or that they are the victims of ideology. The reduction of crime is, after all, a rational concern. It would be more accurate to say that the ingenuity of being "antigraffiti" lies in its ability to exploit the gap between interests that are not mutually inclusive. That is, antigraffiti rhetoric and practice is a deliberately ambiguous entity that places those subject to its logic in a paradoxical situation: with the left hand it holds out safety and security, but with the right hand it takes away all that is presupposed by, and necessary for, the meaningful enjoyment of such safety. In other words, while marginal social groups are invited to support efforts that are purported to increase their personal

---

[82] Squires, "Partnership" (2011).

well-being, they simultaneously support a growth machine that betrays their interest in continuing to reside within their community and city.

## Being Antigraffiti: An Ideology for All Seasons

Focusing on representational practices, disproportionate responses, and political rhetoric, the last two chapters demonstrate that the moral panic concept can be used to map the official reaction to graffiti in New York City and that particular structural dynamics drive such a response. More specifically, they suggest that the rise of neoliberalism and the economic imperatives associated with urban growth machines constitute the major driving forces behind such a response.

The emphasis on neoliberalism is not necessarily at odds with the work of Ferrell and Austin, who have also explored the macro social forces behind official reactions to graffiti. Nils Christie once said that we can exploit crime as much or as little as need, analogizing it to a "limitless natural resource."[83] Like Christie's take on crime, something similar could be said of graffiti writing: For various reasons, powerful groups can exploit the practice at different times and in a multitude of spaces. This is because it opens up possibilities for an antigraffiti rhetoric that, due to its malleability, is compatible with numerous political and economic climates.

The relative powerlessness of graffiti writers enables representations of their culture in which it figures as sinister and threatening, thereby turning them into scapegoats for many kinds of "crisis." As neoliberalism became entrenched, it developed extremely punitive policies to address its related social problems. The intense criminalization of graffiti provides political elites with the type of fodder that allows them to communicate and, more importantly, normalize the draconian penal policies of neoliberalism.

Some of these dynamics are further reflected when one considers reactions to graffiti at the urban level. Here, again, we see that struggles over the meaning of graffiti are dominated by powerful players. Within the urban context, antigraffiti rhetoric mirrors the ideology of privatism. This adversely affects graffiti writers, but more importantly it works against that portion of city residents who, rather than exploit space for economic gain, would much rather develop a meaningful sense of community within their urban environment, a place in which they can *live*. The power of antigraffiti

---

[83] Christie quoted in Worrall, "Rendering Women Punishable" (2002).

rhetoric resides in its ability to hook residents on supporting what appear to be rational, anticrime initiatives while camouflaging how such rhetoric simultaneously serves the interests of landed capital. The problem is that landed capital essentially seeks to commodify urban space, thereby undermining the ability of marginal social groups to remain within the city.

CHAPTER 7

# Conclusion

**Abstract** The concluding chapter summarizes the core arguments of the text and, on this basis, suggests alternative ways in which cities could think about graffiti writing. With a brief look at trends in European urban centers, it is suggested that cities in the USA and other parts of the world would benefit by working with graffiti writers to produce art and murals in shared public spaces. The work ethic of writers could be utilized to minimize state expenditures on graffiti removal and simultaneously enhance the aesthetics of the urban environment. Ending on a fairly pessimistic note, the conclusion acknowledges that the odds of incorporating graffiti into civic life are hampered due to the benefits that political elites see in antigraffiti rhetoric and practice.

**Keywords** Policy · Inclusion · Public art · Ideology · Structure · Barriers · Graffiti

With a particular emphasis on the 1990s and opening years of the twenty-first century, this book offered a social history of graffiti writing culture in New York City. This task was accomplished by isolating two broad trajectories: the history of graffiti writing culture, on the one hand, and the societal response to graffiti on the other. Given that much of the literature in this area has focused on the graffiti that was being painted illegally on the New York City subway system throughout the 1970s and the 1980s, to write about what happened after 1989 amounts to tracing and documenting a span of time hitherto neglected, and hence unwritten. The earlier focus on subway graffiti, as sympathetic as it may have been, has left behind an impression of writing culture in which it figures as a zone of generalized lawlessness and disregard for society's rules. Moreover, we have invariably been encouraged to read graffiti writing as a kind of "resistance." By the mid-1990s, it was becoming clear that these impressions only conveyed a part of the story. As such, this book should be read as one that simultaneously challenges and compliments the work of previous scholars.

During the 1990s, writing culture underwent major changes that were, for the most part, the result of the city's "success" in keeping graffiti off subway trains. To be sure, some graffiti writers do persist in painting trains, but most have gone "above ground." Among the latter, a significant portion has sought out legal avenues in which to pursue their craft. With the production of legal graffiti, writers have shed their anonymity, entered the public square in new and unprecedented ways, and, in some instances, have begun turning once youthful pursuits into adult careers. Moreover, with the turn to legal graffiti, the aesthetic quality of the form has certainly been enhanced.

This legal mode of graffiti production has been accompanied by a new ethos among graffiti writers. Many of the artists who currently paint in the public square lead very conventional lives and embrace socially sanctioned values. They are not unlikely to have families, mortgages, careers, or workplace responsibilities. They buy their spray paint and are often prepared to spend several hundred dollars for the sake of placing murals in public space. Moreover, many display a respect for private property and an acceptance of their society's legal codes—even those that sometimes punish graffiti writers. Most of them, far from seeking exclusion, wish to be embraced and accepted by their social and cultural world.

Of course, this should not be taken to mean that we can go too far in the opposite direction and begin to imagine graffiti writing culture as something that always operates on the permissible side of legality. Nor should we simply imagine graffiti writers as philanthropic altruists free from egoistic impulses. To do so would amount to little more than replacing one partial image with another. However, given the ways in which graffiti has historically been discussed, it is important to start focusing on the new developments within this (sub)culture.

# 7 CONCLUSION

Exploring social responses to graffiti reveals that although some institutions perceive the practice as offering much that is of "value"—be it cultural, political, or economic—this is simply not the case among official agencies devoted to social control. Despite major changes in the structure and practice of graffiti, the official reaction to it, especially in New York City, has remained remarkably consistent for well over four decades. As far as political leaders and the agencies they oversee are concerned, graffiti is simply a "problem" that can only be addressed through repressive and "technological" means.

Legitimated by vehement antigraffiti rhetoric, the city has spent millions of dollars trying to eradicate graffiti over the years. And yet, for all the mobile "power-washing units" that "patrol" New York City, the growing number of city agencies and personnel assigned to "graffiti detail," and the creation of stricter legislation, graffiti remains a prominent feature of the urban landscape. Antigraffiti efforts, far from suppressing anything, simply appear to push graffiti into new urban spaces and force it to adopt new—and sometimes more destructive—forms. This would seem to suggest that the city's efforts are misguided. Indeed, one might be inclined to say that the city stands to benefit by working with graffiti writers. To put it crudely, the city could encourage "good" graffiti (i.e., the "colorful stuff") at the expense of the "ugly" stuff ("tags," "throw-ups"). At present, for example, the city squanders resources to repaint walls and remove graffiti from publicly visible surfaces when they could, as an alternative, utilize the skills and talents of graffiti writers by having them paint elaborate murals on those walls. In short, it may be time to call for a reevaluation of contemporary public policy concerning graffiti in New York City.

To some in New York, other US cities, and those living in regions that have uncritically embraced neoliberal models of social life, such a suggestion may sound incredibly far-fetched, if not irresponsible. Yet, many major European cities, such as Vienna, Prague, Lisbon, and Berlin to name only a few, have created legal walls throughout their urban centers. Of course, this does not stop all forms of illegal graffiti, but it does channel much creative energy into "appropriate," legal outlets. Moreover, when graffiti is encouraged in such a manner, it tends to weave itself into the urban fabric in interesting ways, oftentimes becoming a point of interest for tourists. It is perhaps no accident that European cities tend to respond to graffiti in relatively nuanced ways, which seems to be a legacy of the relationship between writing culture and art worlds. After all, it was segments of the art world that initially introduced writing culture to the

European world, thereby undermining the stigma typically associated with graffiti in much of the USA.

There is evidence to support the claim that those who produce legal murals would be more than receptive to a new approach. To recite "Been3" once more:

> We are not doing anything illegal. We are asking for permission. We are paying for all our own supplies, which is helping the city because we are paying taxes on it of course. Everything they need is being done: They don't have to pay to maintain [walls] because we're maintaining [them]. Also, it makes the neighborhood look better than just having it destroyed. But they don't want us here. They want to get rid of [graffiti].[1]

Legal graffiti writers are frequently known around New York City for their elaborate murals. They often paint murals over walls covered in "tags" and "throw-ups." This tends to keep tags and other forms of graffiti off the walls as people, even other graffiti writers who paint illegally, tend to appreciate the elaborate works. When people do write over the murals, legal graffiti painters are usually willing to go back and create new murals. That is, they tend to maintain the walls with murals.

There are, however, major impediments to the possibility of a cooperative relationship between the city and its legal graffiti writers: Given the imperatives of neoliberalism and the growing desire to commodify urban environments, it makes political sense to insist that graffiti writing culture is a monolithic and destructive entity that "must be opposed." Despite its misleading nature, such a stance provides politicians and other officials with a very effective way to manufacture a "public enemy" that they can deploy to assist in the accomplishment of economic goals and objectives.

As noted, graffiti has been vehemently opposed in New York City for over 40 years, prompting the suggestion that it operates as the irresistible fodder for what is by now a routine "moral panic." In the 1970s and the 1980s, as Hall and colleagues might well have argued had they observed the case, opposition to graffiti effectively deflected attention away from an economic crisis that seriously questioned the desirability of our current political economy. Often articulated in light of the "broken windows"

---

[1] Author's interview with BEEN3.

thesis, contemporary opposition to graffiti works to rationalize the logic of neoliberal state-crafting and the ruthless exploitation of urban space.

While it might seem to be the case that antigraffiti rhetoric is trivial, I would suggest otherwise. Antigraffiti rhetoric and "broken windows" are politically popular frameworks insofar as they offer elites a powerful device that generates widespread public support for a set of economic pursuits that do not necessarily improve the lives of that very public. As I have expressed it, opposition to graffiti currently operates as a mechanism to negotiate the tensions that accompany worsening social and urban exclusion, and which are typically managed through punitive, repressive means.

What such an analysis allows us to see, then, is that the moral panic over graffiti *cannot be reduced to a simple conflict between the city and its graffiti writers*. There are much deeper and much more profound social antagonisms at work here. *These antagonisms revolve around the city's power elite and the city's marginalized groups broadly conceived.*

As far as the graffiti writers of New York City are concerned, it seems that they have several strategies open to them. Through their practice, they could hope to convince the city's public officials that a much more nuanced understanding of graffiti is warranted, one that recognizes writing culture as a complex and ambiguous aesthetic practice. While it certainly has its "illegal" side, it also has a domain that is colorful, vibrant, and therefore capable of harmonizing with public sensibilities. Understanding graffiti writing culture as such would allow the city to make—at the very least—some attempts at directing the energy that the production of graffiti presupposes toward its "legal" and "artistic" poles.

Of course, given the ideological and material usefulness of being "antigraffiti," this strategy seems like wishful thinking. It is, nevertheless, probably better than patiently waiting for the emergence of a new "scapegoat" group, or perhaps a qualitatively different social structure, in the hopes of having the creative energy and output of graffiti writing culture embraced as a constitutive part of civic life.

# Appendix

## Methodological Statement

In the early summer of 2005, I began utilizing ethnographic research methods to address several questions concerning contemporary graffiti writing culture. As an active graffiti writer since 1989, I have seen the subculture experience many new developments and consistently adapt to changing social contexts. I was excited whenever a serious academic study on graffiti was published, and usually enthralled by the reading. However, I began to notice that much of the literature was not addressing the versatility and dynamic nature of graffiti writing culture. I knew graffiti writers were confronted with increasingly severe forms of state opposition and therefore striving to find new avenues of expression, but it seemed that scholars did not find this sociologically interesting. Moving to New Haven to attend Yale University brought me to New York City, which is often regarded as the "birthplace"—or the Mecca—of graffiti throughout the world. As such, it remains the paradigm case for analyzing writing culture.

I began developing a sense of post-1989 graffiti by systematically documenting its more elaborate murals, which can be found throughout New York City. I would take the train to the last stop of each subway line that runs out to the Bronx. I would then get out and walk back in the direction of Manhattan, documenting the graffiti murals as I passed through neighborhoods. Given that only so much ground could be covered per day using this method, it took anywhere from 7 to 14 days to document the area surrounding any given subway line. I repeated this process for most of the train lines that run out to Queens and Brooklyn.

This visual documentation came to be of later importance in several respects. After several months, I had amassed a visual archive of just over 2,000 photographs of graffiti murals in New York City. An analysis of this visual record revealed many cases in which the same individual, and sometimes the same group of individuals, produced many murals. That is, some graffiti artists and some "crews" were much more prolific than others. From here, I created a list, which contained approximately 50 individual "tag" names, of the most prolific artists. I then attempted to interview at least 20 of these individuals. I made contact with graffiti writers in a number of ways. In some instances, the artists, in case anyone wished to procure their creative services, left their phone numbers on the walls they had painted. I simply called the number, informed the artist of my research, and asked if they would like to be interviewed. Most were more than happy to do so. Some of these interviewees put me in contact with other graffiti writers who were on my list. In this manner, I interviewed 15 of the people on my list.

In the course of exploring New York City, I stumbled upon a warehouse located in Long Island City, Queens. The exterior of this warehouse was covered in countless graffiti murals. I soon learned that this building was known as "5Pointz" and was a place where graffiti writers could paint with permission. I began visiting and documenting "5Pointz" on a regular basis, usually several times throughout the week, and on the weekends.

These visits enabled me to meet and have countless informal conversations with many graffiti writers from New York City and throughout the world. Aside from learning about the lives and viewpoints of graffiti writers, these conversations often informed me of graffiti related art shows or events, such as the "Meeting of Styles,"[1] which I often attended and observed. "5Pointz" also provided opportunities to witness the processes involved in creating graffiti-style murals and to observe the ways in which graffiti writers interact when creating large-scale works that involve more than one artist (what the writers refer to as "productions"). After several months of visiting "5Pointz," I had conducted five additional

---

[1] The Meeting of Styles is an event that takes place in many cities around the world on an annual basis. Artists come from many parts of the world to paint legal graffiti murals at such events.

interviews with some of the graffiti writers that I had met there and who happened to be on the list I initially generated.

That I had developed a rapport with many graffiti writers was clear as they soon started telling me when they had plans to paint murals in other parts of the city. I would observe, and sometimes participate in, the creation of these elaborate works. Taken together, all this indicates that "5Pointz" fulfilled many of the functions that ethnographers and qualitative researchers usually attribute to those they call "gatekeepers" of the field.

Although I reached my respondents in different ways, the interviews were conducted in a relatively uniform manner. The interviews, most of which lasted about 1 h, were semistructured. While I had a list of questions and talking points that I always covered, I also let my respondents pursue issues that arose during the course of the interviews. I asked the graffiti writers about their historical involvement with graffiti; their views on past and contemporary graffiti writing cultures; the kinds of encounters they have had with the general public and commercial spheres (e.g., art worlds, advertising, and so on); and about their perceptions concerning the social and political status of graffiti writing in the city.

My 20 respondents—16 men and 4 women—came from a variety of class, "ethnic" and educational backgrounds. They were aged between 22 and 50 with most hovering around 30 years of age. At the time of conducting my interviews, only one respondent had been painting graffiti for less than 10 years (8 years). The other 19 respondents had been involved with graffiti writing culture for at least 10 years. The majority of my interviewees had been painting for around 20 years and two of them for over 30 years. The graffiti writers I spoke to generally started their graffiti careers by painting illegally during their youth, but transitioned to legal graffiti during the 1990s or as they entered their twenties. Some of the younger artists I spoke to, given that they began to write graffiti during the 1990s—a time when legal graffiti was firmly established—had never painted illegally.

The interviews were audio-recorded and then transcribed. The process of transcribing is long and tedious. Yet it did have the advantage of making me intimately familiar with my interview data. It was during the transcribing process that I began to develop an awareness of common patterns, divergences, and unexpected findings in my data. Once I had interview transcripts, I placed them in a file—almost as if to create a text that could lend itself to interpretation—and read them many times.

In reading and rereading my interview material, I tried to learn about the kinds of lives led by my respondents; how they perceived the graffiti they produce; how they view the social structure within which this graffiti is located; and about their sociocultural experiences as graffiti writers. Each time I thought I had developed a theme or idea that accurately captured an aspect of my data, and by extension graffiti writing culture, I reread my interview material and compared transcripts to check for its veracity. This back-and-forth process between idea and data—what some might consider under the rubric of "grounded theory"—generated some very unexpected results. For example, when asking graffiti writers if they thought writing graffiti constituted a political act, I was almost certain that they would all say "oh yes, it is a political act." However, the overwhelming majority of my respondents said the opposite. They assured me that rather than graffiti being political, it was simply something that they enjoyed doing for its own sake. As I often heard it expressed, "we just like to paint."

A second example. When asking graffiti writers how they felt about the commercial uses of graffiti I was expecting to hear a discourse of "authenticity" in which graffiti exchanged for money somehow became "inauthentic," fraudulent. Yet, most of my respondents reported otherwise. Far from rejecting the commercial world and the possibility of earning an income from the selling of their creative talents, they welcomed such opportunities. Many actually wished for greater involvement with commercial arenas from which they could benefit economically.

I cite these two examples because it was during moments such as these that I realized my methods were not simply confirming what I hypothesized to be true, but were forcing me to rethink my a priori beliefs and preconceptions. Insofar as this was the case, I developed a kind of trust in my methods. Having said that, it should also be noted that my sample was not selected randomly and that I did not formally interview all the people I would have liked to. Nevertheless, and in light of the many informal conversations I have had with graffiti writers,[2] I believe that the 20 people I did interview reflect, with some degree of accuracy, the views, values, and so on, of those who produce graffiti with permission in New York City. Although this interview material can be found throughout the book, it ultimately serves as the basis for the Chaps. 3 and 4.

---

[2] That is, informal conversations with graffiti writers who paint legally and illegally.

APPENDIX 137

Alongside observations and interviews, I also consulted a variety of documents. These include newspaper articles from the *New York Times*, the *Daily News*, and independent newspapers such as *The Village Voice*; press releases of the Giuliani and Bloomberg administrations; and other political memos and government reports.

Articles from the *New York Times* and *Daily News* were retrieved from Lexis-Nexis. Using the term "graffiti," I conducted "full text" searches for each individual year from 1990 through to 2005. This period is significant as it is the time over which the new graffiti writing culture emerged and became entrenched. However, in the case of the *Daily News* I could only search from 1995 onward. The articles were then perused and, if deemed to be of some relevance, printed. With much of the "noise" being a product of references to the film "American Graffiti" or the Palm OS "Graffiti" technology, determining the relevance of any given article was a relatively straightforward procedure. In cases of uncertainty, the article was printed and retained. Newspaper articles from other sources, such as *The Village Voice*, were used to supplement this larger body of articles.

Most of the documents from the Giuliani administration were retrieved from the City Hall library in New York City. This would not have been possible without the help of the library staff who provided the information required to locate relevant documents. These included Giuliani's press releases, internal memos, and figures and literature associated with anti-graffiti initiatives. The press releases of the Bloomberg administration were found online (www.nyc.gov). Like the newspaper articles, I read through Bloomberg's press releases and printed those that were seen as relevant to the topic at hand. The New York City government Web site also has a search engine that enabled me to find many other documents related to graffiti, such as those made available by the NYPD and other city agencies.

I ended up with well over 1,500 documents. Approximately 1,100 of these came from the major print media in New York City: there were about 800 articles from the *New York Times* and 300 from the *Daily News*. I discovered 210 relevant documents in the archived papers of Mayor Giuliani and 260 pertinent documents in Mayor Bloomberg's archived papers. I analyzed this entire corpus to make sense of official opposition to graffiti writing in New York City. I was particularly interested in understanding the worldview and material interests held by the political elite, and how this resonated with their vehement opposition to graffiti.

Toward this end, I created five files and arranged their contents in chronological order. The five files were titled: "*The New York Times*" (four folders); "*The Daily News*" (three folders); "Other Print Media"; "Giuliani Files"; and "Bloomberg Files." Having organized the documents into files, I then conducted a discourse analysis. Like the interview material, I read through my files many times. During the first reading, I simply noted on each document (e.g., a newspaper article) the themes it included. I then created an index based on the themes identified while reading through the files a second time. There were many themes, such as "subway graffiti," "legal graffiti," "antigraffiti legislation," "graffiti removal," "arrest of graffiti writer/s," "graffiti as 'broken window,'" and so on. Each individual document/article was then listed according to its content. In cases where an article contained, say, for example, two themes, it was listed under both theme headings. Having such an index not only provided an accessible overview of what my sources contained, but also allowed me to identify the themes that recurred with greater and lesser frequency within the discourse on graffiti. Although I did not attempt to quantify my sources in any way, it was apparent that the majority of the documents I had gathered contained sentiments and recorded official activity that displayed a clear opposition to graffiti. It is worth noting here that although there were obviously some articles that defended graffiti or spoke of it in a positive manner, these articles were usually "balanced" by an official spokesperson that opposed graffiti. Interestingly, articles that simply denounced graffiti often felt no need to seek a "balance" by incorporating opposing viewpoints.

In light of these observations, I decided to reread my articles and create two new indexes. The first index provided an overview of "balanced" reports. Here, earlier categories, such as "legal graffiti," were broken down to include more specific themes. Among these were included "graffiti as 'art,'" "graffiti in advertising," "graffiti as fashion," and so on. Many of these articles were used to add further substance to the interview material offered in Chap. 3.

The second index sought to provide an overview of the official reaction to graffiti. Once again, some new themes emerged here. I began by drawing a distinction between "discursive" and "material" responses to graffiti. Each of these categories contained further subcategories. Having compartmentalized my documents I began rereading them to derive clear answers to two deceptively straightforward questions. First, how can the official reaction to graffiti be described? And, second, how can the official response to graffiti be explained? Paralleling the method used when analyzing the interview material, each time I thought I had found answers to these questions within my documents, I would check their plausibility against a rereading of my (documentary) sources. This back-and-forth process occurred several times before I settled on the results offered in Chaps. 5 and 6.

# BIBLIOGRAPHY

Adorno, Theodor, and Max Horkheimer. *Dialectic of Enlightenment: Philosophical Fragments.* Translated by Edmund Jephcott. Stanford: Stanford University Press, 2002.

Ahearn, Charlie, and Fred Brathwaite. *Wild Style.* Los Angeles, CA: Rhino/Time Warner, 82 minutes, 1982.

Austin, Joe. *Taking the Train: How Graffiti Art Became an Urban Crisis in New York City.* New York: Columbia University Press, 2001.

Austin, Joe. "More to See than a Canvas in a White Cube: For an Art in the Streets." *City* 14, no. 1–2 (2010): 33–47.

Ayres Jr., B. Drummond. "In a City of Graffiti, Gangs Turn to Violence to Protect Their Art." *New York Times,* March 13, 1994: Section 1, 20.

Barnes, Julian E. "Mural Painters Arrested but then Released." *New York Times,* February 10, 2000: B3.

Bass, Sharon L. "For Graffiti Artists, Tough Critics and a Counter-offensive." *New York Times,* August 24, 1986: Section 11CN, 2.

Bayliss, Sarah. "Museum With (Only) Walls." *New York Times,* August 8, 2004: Section 2, 26.

Becker, Howard. *Art Worlds.* Berkeley: University of California Press, 1982.

Belafonte, Harry, and David V. Picker. *Beat Street.* Directed by Stan Lathan. Santa Monica, CA: MGM, 106 minutes, 1984.

Belluck, Pam. "Graffiti Maker 'Cost,' a Prankster to Some but a Criminal in the Law's Eyes, Is Sentenced." *New York Times,* June 29, 1995: B3.

Bennet, James. "A New Arsenal of Weapons to Tag Graffiti Artists." *New York Times,* September 27, 1992: Section 4, 2.

Berger, Joseph. "An Uphill Battle Against Roadside Squalor." *New York Times,* April 28, 1990: 27.

© The Author(s) 2017
R. Kramer, *The Rise of Legal Graffiti Writing in New York and Beyond*, DOI 10.1007/978-981-10-2800-7

Bertrand, Donald. "Graffiti-Busters Tag Rudy for Aid." *Daily News*, September 19, 1995: Suburban, 3.
Bertrand, Donald. "Graffiti Vandals Unpainting the Town." *Daily News*, May 21, 1997: Suburban, 1.
Bertrand, Donald. "Flushing Strip Giving Graffiti the Brushoff." *Daily News*, April 23, 2003: Suburban, 4.
Bertrand, Donald. "Tough Justice Demanded After Graffiti Spree." *Daily News*, January 6, 2004: Suburban, 1.
Bloomberg Files. "Mayor Michael R. Bloomberg Announces 'Operation Silent Night.'" Press Release # 257-02. October 2, 2002a. [All Bloomberg Files are from: www.nyc.gov.]
Bloomberg Files. "Improving Our Quality of Life: Operation Silent Night." Open Letter, October 7, 2002b.
Bloomberg Files. "Mayor Michael R. Bloomberg Delivers 2003 State of the City Address." Press Release # 024-03. January 23, 2003a.
Bloomberg Files. "Mayor Michael R. Bloomberg Announces Queen's Plaza Clean-up to Improve Quality of Life and Promote Economic Development." Press Release # 056-03. February 25, 2003b.
Bloomberg Files. "Driving Crime Down and Revitalizing Neighborhoods Throughout the City." Open Letter. June 22, 2003c.
Bloomberg Files. "Mayor Bloomberg Updates Citywide Graffiti Cleanup Initiative." Press Release # 195-03. July 16, 2003d.
Bloomberg Files. "Making Our City Stronger Neighborhood by Neighborhood." Public Address. July 20, 2003e.
Bloomberg Files. "2004 State of the City Address by Michael R. Bloomberg." Transcript of State of the City Address. January 8, 2004a.
Bloomberg Files. "Mayor Michael R. Bloomberg Announces Historic Crime Reduction in 2004." Press Release # 345-04. December 13, 2004b.
Bloomberg Files. "Mayor Michael R. Bloomberg and Police Commissioner Raymond W. Kelly Re-Launch 'Operation Impact.'" Press Release # 021-05. January 13, 2005a.
Bloomberg Files. "Mayor Bloomberg Discusses Crime Reduction Strategies at Citizen's Crime Commission Breakfast." Press Release # 168-05. May 2, 2005b.
Bloomberg Files. "Mayor Bloomberg Signs Legislation to Fight Graffiti." Press Release # 486-05. December 29, 2005c.
Bloomberg Files. "Mayor Michael R. Bloomberg Delivers 2006 State of the City Address." Press Release # 030-06. January 26, 2006.
Braverman, Harry. *Labor and Monopoly Capital: The Degradation of Work in the Twentieth Century*. New York: Monthly Review Press, 1974.
Brenner, Elsa. "Combating the Spread of Graffiti." *New York Times*, May 30, 1993.

Browne, Malcolm W. "Laser Weapon Obliterates Graffiti, Not Missiles." *New York Times*, April 21, 1996: Section 1, 36.

Buckley, Cara, and Marc Santora. "Night Falls, and 5Pointz, a Graffiti Mecca, is Whited Out in Queens." *New York Times*, November 19, 2013. Accessed on July 27, 2016: http://www.nytimes.com/2013/11/20/nyregion/5pointz-a-graffiti-mecca-in-queens-is-wiped-clean-overnight.html?_r=0

Butterfield, Fox. "On New York Walls, The Fading of Graffiti." *New York Times*, May 6, 1988: B1.

Campos, Ricardo. "Graffiti Writer as Superhero." *European Journal of Cultural Studies* 16, no. 2 (2012): 155–170.

Castleman, Craig. *Getting Up: Subway Graffiti in New York*. Cambridge, MA: MIT Press, 1982.

Chambliss, William, and Milton Mankoff. *Whose Law? What Order?* New York: John Wiley, 1976.

Chang, Jeff. *Can't Stop Won't Stop: A History of the Hip-Hop Culture*. New York: St Martin's Press, 2005.

Cohen, Patricia. "Oops, Sorry, Seems that My Pie Chart is Half-Baked." *New York Times*, April 8, 2000: B7.

Cohen, Stanley. *Folk Devils and Moral Panics: The Creation of the Mods and Rockers*. London: MacGibbon and Kee, 1972.

Colangelo, Lisa L. "Mike Signs Noise Bill and 26 Others." *Daily News*, December 30, 2005: 18.

Cooper, Martha, and Henry Chalfant. *Subway Art*. London: Thames and Hudson, 1984.

Corman, Hope, and Naci Mocan. "Carrots, Sticks and Broken Windows." *Journal of Law and Economics* 48 (2005): 235–266.

Crane, Diana. *The Transformation of the Avant-garde: The New York Art World, 1940–1985*. Chicago: University of Chicago Press, 1987.

Daley, Suzanne. "City Subways on the Mend, Gunn Reports." *New York Times*, July 17, 1985: B1.

Davis, Mike. *City of Quartz: Excavating the Future in Los Angeles*. London: Verso, 1990.

Davis, Mike. *Dead Cities and Other Tales*. New York: The Free Press, 2002.

Derrida, Jacques. *The Animal That Therefore I Am*. Translated by David Wills. New York: Fordham University Press, 2008.

Donohue, Pete. "TA Battle Plan for Scratchiti: Cars to Get Plastic Shields." *Daily News*, January 12, 2000a: 6.

Donohue, Pete. "Shiny New Subway Cars Are Marred by Vandals." *Daily News*, October 4, 2000b: 8.

Donohue, Pete. "Transit Cops' Camera Turning Up the Heat." *Daily News*, May 10, 2001: 17.

Donohue, Pete. "Cops: Graffiti King Back, Infamous Tagger's 'DESA' Moniker Spotted." *Daily News*, January 14, 2002a: 10.

Donohue, Pete. "Losing the War on Scratchiti: Subway Window Vandals Frustrate City." *Daily News*, January 29, 2002b: 24.

Donohue, Pete, John Marzulli, and Wendell Jamieson. "New Brush with the Law, Cops Sign Off Graffiti Artist Again." *Daily News*, January 19, 1996: 6.

Douglas, Carlyle C., and Mary Connelly. "Riding Cleaner, If Not Faster." *New York Times*, June 15, 1986: Section 4, 7.

Douglas, Carlyle, C., Mary Connelly, and Laura Mansnerus. "Wondering Where the Graffiti Went?" *New York Times*, October 12, 1986: Section 4, 7.

Douglas, Mary. *Purity and Danger: An Analysis of the Concepts of Pollution and Taboo*. London: Ark Paperbacks, 1984.

Durkheim, Emile. *The Division of Labor in Society*. Glencoe: Free Press, 1960.

Eco, Umberto. *Travels in Hyper Reality*. Orlando, FL: Harcourt Brace Jovanovich, 1986.

Editorial. "Gaining on Graffiti." *New York Times*, October 23, 1986: A26.

Editorial. "The Man Who Saved the Subways." *New York Times*, January 8, 1990a: A16.

Editorial. "New York Transit, Back on Track." *New York Times*, November 27, 1990b: A22.

Editorial. "A Flogging in Singapore." *New York Times*, April 2, 1994: Section 1, 18.

Editorial. "Shoot Down Hostos' Golden Parachute." *Daily News*, December 30, 1997: 24.

Engels, Mary. "S.I. to Get Graffiti-Cleaning Crew." *Daily News*, March 27, 2001: Suburban, 2.

Erikson, Kai. *Wayward Puritans: A Study in the Sociology of Deviance*. New York: John Wiley and Sons, Inc., 1966.

Fairfield, Hannah. "A Meltdown in the Subways, But It's Not What You Think." *New York Times*, April 16, 2000: Section 14, 6.

Farrelly, Kevin J. "Graffiti Come Out of Subway into Light of Day." *New York Times*, June 10, 1989: Section 1, 26.

Feeley, Malcolm, and Jonathan Simon. "The New Penology: Notes on the Emerging Strategy of Corrections and Its Implications." *Criminology* 30, no. 4 (1992): 449–474.

Ferrell, Jeff. *Crimes of Style: Urban Graffiti and the Politics of Criminality*. Boston, MA: Northeastern University Press, 1993.

Ferris, Marc. "Graffiti as Art. As a Gang Tag. As a Mess." *New York Times*, September 8, 2002: Section 14WC, 1.

Freud, Sigmund. *Civilization and Its Discontents*. Translated by James Strachey. New York: W.W. Norton and Company, 1961.

Gardiner, Sean. "KIKO Was Here." *The Village Voice*, February 28–March 6, 2007: 16.
Gastman, Roger, Darin Rowland, and Ian Sattler. *Freight Train Graffiti*. New York: Harry N. Abrams, Inc., 2006.
George, Nelson. *Hip Hop America*. New York: Viking, 1998.
Gitlin, Todd. "Movies of the Week." In *Rethinking Popular Culture: Contemporary Perspectives in Cultural Studies*, edited by C. Mukerji and M. Schudson, 335–356. Berkeley: University of California Press, 1991.
Giuliani Files. "Mayor Giuliani Kicks Off Adopt-A-Highway Maintenance Provider Program." Press Release # 124-95. From Giuliani Papers, Office of the Mayor, Folder Title: March 1995. Location: Folder # 16511; Roll # 60276. March 23, 1995a.
Giuliani Files. "Mayor Giuliani Removes Graffiti from Queensborough Bridge." Press Release # 375-95. From Giuliani Papers, Office of the Mayor, Folder Title: Anti-Graffiti Task Force—Executive Order. Location: Folder # 4676, NYC Municipal Archives. July 10, 1995b.
Giuliani Files. "Executive Order No. 24, Mayor's Anti-Graffiti Task Force." Found in Folder Title: *Police Department—Graffiti*. Location: Folder # 0141; Roll # 60696, NYC Municipal Archives. July 11, 1995c.
Giuliani Files. "Mayor Giuliani Presents Proclamation to We Care About New York." Press release # 455-95. From Giuliani Papers, Office of the Mayor, Folder Title: August 1995. Location: Folder # 16516; Roll # 60276. August 21, 1995d.
Giuliani Files. "Mayor Giuliani Announced Community Anti-Graffiti Clean Ups in Staten Island, Gramercy Park, and East Harlem." Press Release # 599-95. From Giuliani Papers, Office of the Mayor, Folder Title: November 1995. Location: Folder # 16519; Roll # 60276. November 6, 1995e.
Giuliani Files. "Anti-Graffiti Expo '96." Found in Folder Title: *Police Department—Graffiti*. Location: Folder # 0141; Roll # 60696, NYC Municipal Archives. 1996.
Giuliani Files. "Mayor Giuliani Continues Assault on Graffiti as City Targets Several Neighborhoods for Cleanup." Press Release # 446-98. September 26, 1998.
Glickman, Joe. "Weekend Warrior: Stalking the Bear (Bears Optional)." *New York Times*, June 9, 2000: Section E, 33.
Gonzalez, David. "Legal Graffiti? The Police Voice Dissent." *New York Times*, September 11, 1996: B1.
Goode, Erich, and Nachman Ben-Yehuda. *Moral Panics: The Social Construction of Deviance*. Oxford: Blackwell, 1994.
Goodman, Ari L. "Dogs to Patrol Subway Yards." *New York Times*, September 15, 1981a: A1.

Goodman, Ari L. "City to Use Pits of Barbed Wire in Graffiti War." *New York Times*, December 15, 1981b: B1.

Gottdiener, Mark. *The Theming of America: American Dreams, Media Fantasies, and Themed Environments*. Colorado: Westview Press, 2001.

Haberman, Clyde. "Graffiti Wars in the Subway: It's Round 2." *New York Times*, December 19, 1995: B1.

Haberman, Clyde. "Graffiti 'Art'? Issue Deserves a Sharp Stake." *New York Times*, October 22, 1996: B1.

Haberman, Clyde. "In Subways, Vandals Etch Old Defiance." *New York Times*, August 19, 1997: B1.

Haberman, Clyde. "New Vandals Scratching Up the Subways." *New York Times*, January 26, 1999: B1.

Hager, Steven. *Hip Hop: The Illustrated History of Break Dancing, Rap Music, and Graffiti*. New York: St Martin's Press, 1984.

Haitch, Richard. "Thwarting Graffiti." *New York Times*, October 24, 1982: Section 1, 42.

Hall, Stuart, and Tony Jefferson. *Resistance Through Rituals: Youth Subcultures in Post-war Britain*. London: Hutchinson, 1976.

Hall, Stuart, Chas Critcher, Tony Jefferson, John Clarke, and Brian Roberts. *Policing the Crisis: Mugging, the State, and Law and Order*. New York: Holmes & Meier Publishers, Inc, 1978.

Halsey, Mark, and Alison Young. "Our Desires Are Ungovernable: Writing Graffiti in Urban Space." *Theoretical Criminology* 10, no. 3 (2006): 275–306.

Hanley, Robert. "Police Squad Pursues North Bergen Graffiti Vandals." *New York Times*, April 12, 1995: B6.

Harcourt, Bernard E. "Reflecting on the Subject: A Critique of the Social Influence Conception of Deterrence, the Broken Windows Theory, and Order-maintenance Policing New York Style." *Michigan Law Review* 97 (1998): 299–398.

Harcourt, Bernard E. *Illusion of Order: The False Promise of Broken Windows Policing*. Cambridge, MA: Harvard University Press, 2001.

Harcourt, Bernard E., and Jens Ludwig. "Broken Windows: New Evidence from New York City and a Five-city Social Experiment." *University of Chicago Law Review* 73, no. 1 (2006): 271–320.

Hays, Constance L. "Transit Agency Says New York Subways Are Free of Graffiti." *New York Times*, May 10, 1989: A1.

Hebdidge, Dick. *Subculture: The Meaning of Style*. London: Routledge, 1979.

Herman, Robin. "Vandals Take Psychological Toll." *New York Times*, May 21, 1971: A1.

Hernandez, Raymond. "Police Scope Out Night Writers." *New York Times*, October 3, 1993: Section 13, 12.

Hirsch, Paul. "Processing Fads and Fashions: An Organization-set Analysis of Cultural Industry Systems." *American Journal of Sociology* 77 (1972): 639–659.

Hurley, Dan. "Scientists at Work—Fenton Earls: On Crime as Science." *New York Times*, January 6, 2004: F1.

Hutcheon, Stephen, Louisa Hearn, and David Braithwaite. "Australia Bans Graffiti Game." *Sydney Morning Herald*, February 16, 2006. Accessed on July 27, 2016: http://www.smh.com.au/news/breaking/graffiti-game-banned-in-australia/2006/02/15/1139890798010.html.

James, George. "Goggles Brighten Dark Subway." *New York Times*, April 10, 1992: B2.

Jochnowitz, George. "Manhattan Transfer." Letter to the Editor, *New York Times*, February 13, 2000: Section 6, 10.

Kelling, George L., and William J. Bratton. "Declining Crime Rates: Insiders' Views of the New York City Story." *Journal of Criminal Law and Criminology* 88 (1998): 1217–1231.

Kelly, Raymond. "The NYPD Strategic Approach to Stopping Graffiti Vandalism." *The Police Chief* 72, no. 8 (August 2005): np. Accessed on July 26, 2016:. http://www.policechiefmagazine.org.

Kleinfield, N. R. "Bay Ridge Begins to Fear Its Youth." *New York Times*, October 5, 1994: B2.

Kocieniewski, David. "One Year Later: New Canvas, Same 'Tag.'" *New York Times*, January 19, 1996: B2.

Kramer, Ronald. "A Social History of Graffiti Writing in New York City, 1990–2005." PhD dissertation, Yale University: Department of Sociology, 2009.

Kramer, Ronald. "Moral Panics and Urban Growth Machines: Official Reactions to Graffiti in New York City, 1990–2005." *Qualitative Sociology* 33, no. 3 (2010): 297–311.

Kramer, Ronald. "Political Elites, 'Broken Windows,' and the Commodification of Urban Space." *Critical Criminology* 20, no. 3 (2012): 229–248.

Kramer, Ronald, Valli Rajah, and Hung-En Sung. "Neoliberal Prisons and Cognitive Treatment: Calibrating the Subjectivity of Incarcerated Young Men to Economic Inequalities." *Theoretical Criminology* 17, no. 4 (2013): 535–556.

Krauss, Clifford. "Decoding Graffiti to Solve Bigger Crimes; Police Experts Identifying Gangs, Feuds, Drugs and Personal Signatures." *New York Times*, October 4, 1996: B1.

Lachmann, Richard. "Graffiti as Career and Ideology." *American Journal of Sociology* 94, no. 2 (1988): 229–250.

La Ferla, Ruth. "CK One's New Motif." *New York Times*, May 6, 2003: Section 13, 8.

Lambert, Bruce. "New Blight: Scratches as Graffiti." *New York Times*, January 23, 1994: Section 13, 6.
Lemire, Jonathan. "Graffiti Kids Tagged Out, Cleanup Tied to Lower Crime." *Daily News*, June 3, 2002a: Suburban, 1.
Lemire, Jonathan. "Cops Wiping Out Graffiti." *Daily News*, June 9, 2002b: Suburban, 3.
Lemire, Jonathan. "Frontal Attack on Graffiti: Pol Urges Businesses, Residents to Join Effort." *Daily News*, October 27, 2003: Suburban, 1.
Levine, Richard. "Transit Authority Proclaims a Success: 50% of Cars Clean." *New York Times*, October 6, 1986: B1.
Licata, Paula Canzi. "Midnight Writers Defacing the L.I.E." *New York Times*, June 11, 1989: Section 12LI, 32.
Logan, John R., and Harvey Molotch. *Urban Fortunes: The Political Economy of Place*. Los Angeles, CA: University of California Press, 1987.
Lombardi, Frank. "City Gives the Brushoff to Graffiti Party Permit." *Daily News*, August 16, 2005: 2.
Louie, Elaine. "Who You Gonna Call? Graffitibusters!" *New York Times*, October 8, 1998: Section F, 3.
MacDiarmid, Laura, and Steven Downing. "A Rough Aging Out: Graffiti Writers and Subcultural Drift." *International Journal of Criminal Justice Sciences* 7, no. 2 (2012): 605–617.
Macdonald, Dwight. "A Theory of Mass Culture." In *Mass Culture: The Popular Arts in America*, edited by B. Rosenberg and D. W. White, 59–73. New York: Macmillan, 1957.
Macdonald, Nancy. *The Graffiti Subculture: Youth, Masculinity and Identity in London and New York*. Basingstoke: Palgrave Macmillan, 2001.
MacDowall, Lachlan. "#Instafame: Aesthetics, Audiences, Data." In *Graffiti and Street Art: Reading, Writing and Representing the City*, edited by K. Avramidis and M. Tsilimpounidi. London: Routledge, 2016. forthcoming.
Mailer, Norman. *The Faith of Graffiti. With Photographs by Mervyn Kurlansky and Jon Naar*. New York: Praeger, 1974.
Marcano, Tony. "TATS Cru Wins Coca-Cola Account." *New York Times*, April 16, 1995: Section 13, 4.
Marriott, Michael. "Too Legit to Quit." *New York Times*, October 3, 1993: Section 13, 4.
Martin, Richard A. "The Rebirth of the New York Sneakerhead." *New York Times*, July 11, 2004: Section 14, 4.
Massey, Douglas S., and Nancy A. Denton. *American Apartheid: Segregation and the Making of the Underclass*. Cambridge, MA: Harvard University Press, 1993.
McDonell, Nick. "A Graffiti War with Pol." *Daily News*, July 3, 2005: 47.

Melago, Carrie. "Riled Pol Tags *Time* Mag Ad." *Daily News*, June 30, 2005a: 23.
Melago, Carrie. "Pol Sees Red Over Graffiti Party." *Daily News*, August 15, 2005b: 6.
Miles, Martha A. "In the Subway a Measure of Control Is Up." *New York Times*, May 14, 1989: Section 4, 24.
Miller, Ivor. *Aerosol Kingdom: Subway Painters of New York City*. Jackson: University Press of Mississippi, 2002.
Mincer, Jilian. "Is the Transit Authority Winning the War on Grime?" *New York Times*, November 24, 1985: 24.
Mitchell, Donald. *The Right to the City: Social Justice and the Fight for Public Space*. New York: Guildford Press, 2003.
Mooney, Jake. "Times Magazine Gets Down with It." *New York Times*, June 26, 2005: Section 14, 5.
Muro, Matt. "He Discovered the Antidote to Pharmacy School." *New York Times*, September 2, 2001: Section 14, 3.
Murray, James, and Karla Murray. *Broken Windows: Graffiti NYC*. Gingko Press, 2002.
Ogawa, Jillian. "Graffiti Busters to Target Sunnyside." *Daily News*, May 6, 2005: Suburban, 4.
Olmeda, Rafael A. "Tide Turns vs. Crime at Project: Three Month Campaign Cited." *Daily News*, August 25, 1995: Suburban, 39.
Onishi, Norimitsu. "Finally, That's All He Wrote." *New York Times*, November 20, 1994: Section 13, 10.
Perez, Luis. "Boro Giving Brush-Off to Graffiti." *Daily News*, May 20, 2003: Suburban, 1.
Peterson, Helen. "Ecko Designs Bloomy Suit." *Daily News*, August 19, 2005a: 14.
Peterson, Helen. "Party Is On! Graffiti Ban Overruled." *Daily News*, August 23, 2005b: 7.
Phillips, Susan. *Wallbangin': Graffiti and Gangs in L.A.* Chicago, IL: University of Chicago Press, 1999.
Pollack, Christopher B. "Islip Moving Against Graffiti." *New York Times*, December 15, 1985: 20.
Powers, Stephen. *The Art of Getting Over: Graffiti at the Millennium*. New York: St. Martin's Press, 1999.
Pratt, John, and Anna Eriksson. *Contrasts in Punishment: An Explanation of Anglophone Excess and Nordic Exceptionalism*. London: Routledge, 2013.
Preston, Julia. "Planner of Graffiti-Themed Event Sues Mayor Bloomberg." *New York Times*, August 20, 2005: B3.
Quintanilla, Blanca M. "Cops in It for Long Scrawl." *Daily News*, October 1, 1995: Suburban, 1.
Rahn, Janice. *Painting Without Permission: Hip-Hop Graffiti Subculture*. Westport, CT: Bergin and Garvey, 2002.

Rajah, Valli, Ronald Kramer, and Hung-En Sung. "Changing Narrative Accounts: How Young Men Tell Different Stories When Arrested, Enduring Jail Time and Navigating Community Reentry." *Punishment & Society* 16, no. 3 (2014): 285–304.

Rein, Lisa, William K. Rashbaum, Ian Michaels, and Gene Mustaine. "A Real Pain in the Glass: Vandals Marring Trains' Windows with 'Scratchiti.'" *Daily News*, May 6, 1996: 8.

Richtel, Matt. "Sony Got Hip, but the Hipsters Got Sony." *New York Times*, December 12, 2005: Section C, 8.

Rose, Tricia. *Black Noise: Rap Music and Black Culture in Contemporary America*. Hanover, NH: Wesleyan University Press, 1994.

Ross, Jeffrey Ian. "Graffiti Goes to the Movies: American Fictional Films Featuring Graffiti Artists/Writers and Themes." *Contemporary Justice Review* 18, no. 3 (2015): 366–383.

Ross, Jeffrey Ian. "How American Movies Depict Graffiti and Street Art." In *Routledge Handbook of Graffiti and Street Art*, edited by J.I. Ross, 429–439. London: Routledge, 2016.

Ross, Jeffrey Ian, and Benjamin S. Wright. "'I've Got Better Things to Worry About': Police Perceptions of Graffiti and Street Art in a Large Mid-Atlantic City." *Police Quarterly* 17, no. 2 (2014): 176–200.

Ruiz, Albor. "Graffiti Phactory Fights Vandal Tag." *Daily News*, April 20, 1998: Suburban, 4.

Rusche, Georg, and Otto Kirchheimer. *Punishment and Social Structure*. New York: Russell and Russell, 1939/1968.

Rutenberg, James. "TA Eyes Camera Plan to Scratch Vandals." *Daily News*, August 13, 1998: 9.

Rutenberg, Jim. "City Revokes Party Permit over Exhibit with Graffiti." *New York Times*, August 16, 2005: B5.

Safire, William. "Crime in Singapore." *New York Times*, April 7, 1994: A27.

Sampson, Robert J., and Stephen W. Raudenbush. "Systematic Social Observation of Public Spaces: A New Look at Disorder in Urban Neighborhoods." *American Journal of Sociology* 105 (1999): 603–637.

Sassen, Saskia. *The Global City: New York, London, Tokyo*. Princeton, NJ: Princeton University Press, 2001.

Saul, Michael. "Mike Vows to Rub Out Graffiti All over Town." *Daily News*, July 11, 2002: Suburban, 1.

Saul, Michael. "Graffiti Bust Not Political, Says Mayor." *Daily News*, October 9, 2003: 38.

Schmidlapp, David, and Phase2. *Style Writing from the Underground: (R)evolution of Aerosol Linguistics*. Terni, Italy: Stampa Alternativa/IGTimes, 1996.

Schwartzman, Allan. *Street Art*. New York: Dial Press, 1985.

Sclafani, Tony. "NYPD's Can-Do War vs. Graffiti, Arming Cops with Digital Cameras Fuels Spike in Vandalism Arrests." *Daily News*, November 14, 2005a: 19.

Sclafani, Tony. "Spray It Ain't So, Graffiti Menace Doubles." *Daily News*, November 25, 2005b: Suburban, 46.

Seifman, David. "Rudy Will Educate Graffiti Vandals." *New York Post*, November 17, 1994: 20.

Shelden, Randall G., and William B. Brown. "The Crime Control Industry and the Management of the Surplus Population." *Critical Criminology* 9, no. 1/2 (2000): 39–62.

Sherman, Rachel. *Class Acts: Service and Inequality in Luxury Hotels*. Berkeley: University of California Press, 2007.

Silver, Tony, and Henry Chalfant. *Style Wars*. Los Angeles, CA: Public Art Films: 70 minutes, 1983/re-released 2004.

Sites, William. *Remaking New York: Primitive Globalization and the Politics of Urban Community*. Minneapolis: University of Minnesota Press, 2003.

Smith, Neil. *The New Urban Frontier: Gentrification and the Revanchist City*. London: Routledge, 1996.

Smothers, Ronald. "Koch Calls for Dogs in Fight on Graffiti." *New York Times*, August 27, 1980: B3.

Snyder, Gregory. *Graffiti Lives: Beyond the Tag in New York's Urban Underground*. New York: New York University Press, 2009.

Sorkin, Michael. *Variations on a Theme Park: The New American City and the End of Public Space*. New York: Hill and Wang, 1992.

Spitz, Ellen H. *Image and Insight: Essays in Psychoanalysis and the Arts*. New York: Columbia University Press, 1991.

Squires, Gregory. "Partnership and the Pursuit of the Private City." In *Readings in Urban Theory*, edited by S. S. Fainstein and S. Campbell, 207–228. West Sussex, UK: Wiley-Blackwell, 2011.

Stewart, Jack. "Subway Graffiti: An Aesthetic Study of Graffiti on the Subway System of New York City, 1970–1978." PhD dissertation, New York University, 1989.

Stewart, Susan. "Ceci Tuera Cela: Graffiti as Crime and Art." In *Life After Postmodernism: Essays on Value and Culture*, edited by J. Fekete, 161–180. New York: St. Martin's Press, 1987.

St. Jean, Peter K. B. *Pockets of Crime: Broken Windows, Collective Efficacy, and the Criminal Point of View*. Chicago: The University of Chicago Press, 2007.

Stokes, Robert J. "Business Improvement Districts and Inner City Revitalization: The Case of Philadelphia's Frankford Special Services District." *International Journal of Public Administration* 29 (2006): 173–186.

Strom, Stephanie. "A Transit Official Outlines Big Cuts." *New York Times*, March 31, 1991: 21.

"'TAKI 183' Spawns Pen Pals." *New York Times*, July 21, 1971: 37.
Tavernise, Sabrina. "Citing 1st Amendment, Judge Says City Must Allow Graffiti Party." *New York Times*, August 23, 2005: B1.
Taylor, Ralph B. *Breaking Away from Broken Windows: Baltimore Neighborhoods and the Nationwide Fight Against Crime, Grime, Fear, and Decline*. Boulder: Westview Press, 2001.
Terry, Don. "Cleaning Graffiti-Scarred Areas, a Wall at a Time." *New York Times*, October 20, 2000: A18.
Thompson, Kenneth. *Moral Panics*. London: Routledge, 1998.
Urry, John. *The Tourist Gaze: Leisure and Travel in Contemporary Societies*. London: Sage, 1990.
Vandam, Jeff. "Thoughts on a Clear Pane." *New York Times*, September 12, 2004: Section 14, 10.
van Loon, Jannes. "'Just Writing Your Name?' An Analysis of the Spatial Behaviour of Graffiti Writers in Amsterdam." *Belgeo* 3 (2014): 1–17.
Wacquant, Loic. *Prisons of Poverty*. Minneapolis, MN: University of Minnesota Press, 2009a.
Wacquant, Loic. *Punishing the Poor: The Neoliberal Government of Social Insecurity*. Durham, NC: Duke University Press, 2009b.
Wacquant, Loic. "Crafting the Neoliberal State: Workfare, Prisonfare, and SocialInsecurity." *Sociological Forum* 25, no. 2 (2010): 197–220.
Walde, Claudia. *Sticker City: Paper Graffiti Art*. London: Thames and Hudson, 2007.
Walsh, R. W. "Union Square Park: From Blight to Bloom." *Economic Development Journal* 5, no. 2 (2006): 38–46.
Ward, Kevin. "'Policies in Motion,' Urban Management and State Restructuring: The Trans-local Expansion of Business Improvement Districts." *International Journal of Urban and Regional Research* 30, no. 1 (2006): 54–75.
Watney, Simon. *Policing Desire: Pornogrpahy, AIDS, and the Media*. Minneapolis: University of Minnesota Press, 1987.
Weir, Richard. "Wall Hits a Patron of Graffiti." *New York Times*, February 15, 1998: Section 14, 10.
Whitney, Craig R. "New Plague for London: Graffiti Tags." *New York Times*, October 13, 1988: A9.
Wilson, James Q., and George L. Kelling. "Broken Windows: The Police and Neighborhood Safety." *Atlantic Monthly* 249 (1982): 29–38.
Wilson, William J. *The Truly Disadvantaged: The Inner City, the Underclass, and Public Policy*. Chicago: University of Chicago Press, 1987.
Woodberry Jr., Warren. "Corp. Wins Its Brush vs. Graffiti." *Daily News*, January 17, 2000: Suburban, 1.
Worrall, Anne. "Rendering Women Punishable: The Making of a Penal Crisis." In *Women and Punishment: The Struggle for Justice*, edited by P. Carlen, 47–66. Cullompton: Willan, 2002.

Wright, Robert. "'I'd Sell You Suicide': Pop Music and Moral Panic in the Age of Marilyn Manson." *Popular Music* 19, no. 3 (2000): 365–385.
Yaniv, O. "Spray and Wash in Sunnyside. Trailer Patrols Nabe to Quickly KO Graffiti." *Daily News*, August 3, 2005: Suburban, 2.
Zukin, Sharon. *Landscapes of Power: From Detroit to Disney World*. Berkeley: University of California Press, 1991.

# Index

**A**
Above-ground, 4, 7, 10, 28, 30, 93, 128
Advertising, 29, 62, 68, 72, 97
Aesthetic, 1, 3, 6, 9, 11–13, 15, 16, 19, 21, 22, 26, 27, 32–34, 35, 43–45, 47, 48, 51–54, 62, 66, 68, 69, 72, 73, 76–78, 80, 96–102, 115, 128, 131
Anarchist, 60
Anarchy, 38
Animal, 86–86, 102
*Animal That Therefore I Am, The*, 85, 86n11
Anti-graffiti, 113, 113n47, 114
Appearance, 10, 24–27, 34, 40n24, 52, 75
Art, 11, 22, 29–31, 38, 44, 44n35, 53, 55, 59, 68–70, 73, 80, 115, 116
Artist, 22, 29, 30, 33, 38, 46–49, 51, 53–55, 57, 59, 63, 64n37, 70, 98, 100, 115, 128, 131
*Art for Transit*, 53
Art worlds, 6, 7, 10, 28, 29–34, 55, 61–81, 129
Audience, 30, 31, 34, 42, 106
Authority, 19, 38, 41, 101, 104, 108, 112, 115

**B**
Background, 15, 17, 18, 47, 49, 51
*Beat Street*, 31
Beef, 57
BID (and/or BIDs, Business Improvement Districts), 120
Bloomberg, 98, 100, 101, 115, 121n77, 122
Bombing, 22, 27, 28, 35, 40–44, 51, 55
Break-dancing, 32, 33
Breaking, 32, 33, 107
Broken windows, 24, 25, 67, 76, 90–92, 130, 131
Bronx, 11, 30, 46, 72
Brooklyn, 64
Buff, 21, 22, 48
*Burning New York*, 76

**C**
Camera, 42, 93, 94
Canvas, 21, 22, 29, 30, 48, 58, 68, 98
Capitalism, 8, 104, 107
Caps, 49
Career, 17, 32, 45, 50, 51, 59, 68, 68n14, 96, 120, 128
Car wash, 21
Circulation, 22, 27, 34, 75–80

City, 2–4, 9, 11, 12, 20, 23, 27, 29–34, 36, 38, 40, 42–50, 51, 54, 63, 67, 72, 73, 80, 81, 83, 84, 90, 92, 94, 96–98, 101–102, 104, 109, 113, 115, 123, 127, 129, 130, 131
Class, 2, 3, 5, 6, 8, 38, 39, 51, 80, 105, 107, 108, 111, 119–122
Clean car, 26
Clean-train, 9, 35–60, 62, 68, 69, 71
Cloud, 15–16, 18, 40
Collective conscious, 19, 106
Collective efficacy, 91
Commodification, 5, 34, 73, 75, 104, 109
Communication, 34, 75, 81, 111
Community, 10, 33, 55, 57, 59, 62, 64, 69, 71, 78, 89, 91, 94, 95, 98, 106, 111, 117, 119, 124, 125
Consent, 101, 107, 108, 111
Consumer
 culture, 63, 73, 75, 80
 society, 2, 7, 39, 62, 68–74
Conventional, 4, 7, 36, 51, 53, 59, 61, 84, 91, 128
Convergences, 85, 88
Crack market, 91
Crew (and/or crews), 43, 88, 89
Crime, 23–25, 87, 88, 90–92, 95, 105, 110, 115, 123, 124
Criminality, 87, 99n66
Criminal justice, 5, 84, 102, 110, 119n66
Crisis, 3, 5, 23, 104, 107, 124, 130
Crusade, 9

Crusaders, 85, 86
Cultural capital, 68
Cultural commodity, 70
Cultural media, 6, 10, 29–34, 54
Culture, 1–3, 5, 7–12, 16, 19–22, 28, 30–34, 35, 38–40, 42–45, 54–60, 61–81, 83, 84, 87–89, 96, 98, 109, 110, 124, 127–131
Culture industry, 10, 34

D
Death penalty, 95
Demonization, 90–92
Design features, 16
Desire, 7, 35, 51, 55, 103–125, 130
Deviance, 106, 107, 109
Discourse, 1, 2, 4, 5, 25, 30, 84, 86, 108, 111, 114, 118, 123
Discursive strategy, 85
Disorder, 24, 90, 91, 123
Disproportionality, 90, 102
Diversity, 32, 51, 80
Draconian, 85, 109, 121, 124
Durkheim, 4, 101, 106

E
Economic opportunities, 68, 72
Empirical support, 25, 90
End to end, 55n56
Etch, 27, 28, 40, 41, 51
Ethic, 37, 38, 52, 111
Ethnicity, 51
Ethnography/Ethnographic, 7, 90
Europe, 33, 39, 48, 129–130
European cities, 129

INDEX 157

Evidence, 7, 41, 88, 90, 93, 97, 102, 130
Exaggeration, 4
Exhibits, 30, 69

**F**
Facebook, 75
*Faith of Graffiti, The*, 31
Fame, 12
Fashion, 30, 62, 68, 72, 98
Fay, Michael, 94, 95
Felony, 91
Fences, 20, 25, 40
Field observations, 7
Fine art, 11, 62, 71
5Pointz, 64n7, 65n7, 97
Flickr, 75
Folk devils, 84–89
Force, 3, 6, 9, 27, 34, 40, 83, 93, 96, 109, 113, 114, 124, 129
Foucault, 5, 87
Freight, 43
Freudian, 87

**G**
Gang (and/or gangs), 10, 88, 89
Gateway drug, 111
Gateway penality, 104, 111
Gender, 3
Gentrification, 97, 120, 123
Getting up, 10, 19, 31, 73
Giuliani, 113, 114, 120
Global, 10, 23, 33, 34, 62
Globalization, 75–80
Graffiti
 free, 26, 27, 80, 112
 for hire, 97

removal, 86, 112, 114–116
tourists, 42
Gramsci, 107
Growth machine, 5, 6, 103–125

**H**
Haring (Keith), 30
Hegemonic, 51
Hip-hop, 1, 31–33
Hitting, 43, 55
*Homo Criminalis*, 87
Hostility, 2, 7, 62, 101, 102
Hot, 57, 93

**I**
Ideology, 5, 117, 118, 123, 124–125
Illegal, 4, 7, 36–45, 51, 97, 99, 129, 131
Image, 36, 58, 84, 87, 128
Imprisonment, 93–96, 100
Incarceration, 110
Inequality, 5, 109, 122
Instagram, 75
Internet, 42, 46, 75

**K**
Killing, 55
Koch, Edward, 23, 25, 26

**L**
Labor market, 104, 109, 110–111
Landed capital, 105, 116, 125
Language, 88, 98
Law, 20, 25, 36, 37, 51, 53, 54, 59, 96, 98, 99, 108

Lay-ups, 4, 12, 20, 21
Legal graffiti, 4, 7, 36, 45–49, 51, 59, 61, 66, 80, 96, 99, 102, 128–130
Legislation, 36, 101, 102, 129
Legitimate, 30, 55, 59, 72, 84, 97, 99–101, 106, 107, 119, 129
Lindsay, John, 20, 21, 25, 113
Logo, 62, 68, 72
Long-range, 93, 94

## M
Manhattan, 11, 99
Marginal, 69, 70, 125
Marginalized, 5, 8, 84, 111, 120, 121, 131
Markers, 10, 11, 44
Marx, 107
Mass media, 9–10, 19, 24, 25, 27, 34, 84, 85, 87, 90, 105, 108, 112
Mechanical, 14
Media, 6, 10, 19, 20, 24, 25, 27, 29–34, 63, 75, 83–102, 105, 106, 112
Metaphor, 85, 87
Military, 93, 94, 112
Misdemeanor, 91–92
Misrepresentation, 90
Moral, 9, 33, 105, 106
Moral Panic, 4, 5, 8, 83–102, 104, 108, 124, 130, 131
MTA / Metropolitan Transport Authority, 19–22, 25, 26, 41, 51, 53, 80
Mural, 47, 49

## N
Neoliberal, 5, 8, 103–125, 129, 131
Neoliberalism, 5, 8, 104, 109–116, 117, 124, 130

Neoliberal state-crafting, 5, 104, 109, 110, 116, 131
New York City, 2–6, 11, 12, 20, 23, 27, 29–31, 33, 34, 36, 40, 42–50, 54, 63, 67, 72, 80, 83–102, 113, 115, 123, 124, 127, 129–131
*New York Times*, 11, 19, 20, 72, 94, 95, 112
Night-vision, 93, 94
NOGA, 29
NYPD (New York Police Department), 94, 113–114

## O
Official reactions, 19–29, 124
Officials, 3, 4, 6, 33, 54, 80, 81, 84, 90, 94, 96, 97, 102, 104, 105, 113, 116, 117, 120, 121, 123, 124, 129–131
One-dimensional, 81
Opposition, 2, 6, 36, 38, 51–54, 57, 64, 85, 97–99, 104, 118, 130–131
Outlaw, 60
Outsiders, 2, 39–40, 63, 75
Over-reaction, 4

## P
Paintings, 7, 19, 24, 29, 30–31, 35, 42–43, 45–50, 55, 59, 66, 76, 93, 128
Panel piece, 55n56
Penality, 103–125
Permission, 4, 45–50, 58–60, 66, 96–98
Personal responsibility, 109
Piece, 10–19, 22, 33, 38, 42–45, 47, 49, 55, 88, 101
Political elite, 9, 34, 63, 83–102, 110, 116, 118, 121, 124

INDEX 159

Post-1989, 9, 36, 40, 42
Poverty, 23, 109, 110
Print media, 6, 20, 63, 83–102
Prison, 94–96, 102, 109, 110, 111
Private property, 51, 100, 101, 102, 128
Privatism, 5, 116–124
Production, 30, 35–60, 67, 75, 107, 128, 131
Profit-motive, 75
Property, 4, 5, 8, 46, 49, 51, 100–102, 111, 119–121, 128
Psychological, 24, 95, 102, 120
Public-private partnership, 117, 121
Punishment, 93–95, 100, 102, 109–116
Punitive, 5, 8, 102, 104, 109–116, 124, 131

**Q**
Quality of life, 117
Queens, 97

**R**
Race, 2, 3, 38, 39
Racial segregation, 122
Rap, 32, 33
Rapping, 32, 33
Rebel, 60
Rebellious, 38
Recognition, 10, 11, 29, 42, 43, 46, 69, 70, 85
Repaint, 21, 25, 58, 86, 113, 129
Representation, 15, 20, 27, 84, 90, 102, 124
Residents, 6, 24–27, 32, 117, 119, 125
Resistance, 2, 7, 36–40, 62, 128
Respect, 16, 21, 29, 30, 33, 34, 37, 50–59, 70, 128

Rhetoric, 4, 6, 20, 31, 85, 90, 104, 117, 118, 123–125, 129, 131
Rollie, 44, 45
Rule enforcers, 106

**S**
Sacred, 101
Security, 20, 25, 54, 123
Self-expression, 101
Signification spiragl, 84–89
Singapore, 94–95
Sketch, 17, 48, 67
Social control, 100, 121, 129
Social disadvantage, 6
Softie letters, 14, 17
Solidarity, 104, 106
Space, 3, 5, 6, 17, 24, 27, 29, 30, 33, 35–60, 69, 71, 80, 91, 102, 104, 120, 121, 123, 124
*Spraycan Art*, 31, 33
Spray paint, 20, 21, 40, 44, 48, 49, 53, 67, 94, 128
State-crafting, 5, 104, 109, 110, 116, 131
Status, 2, 57, 60, 69, 90
Stencils, 44
Sticker culture, 44
Stickers, 44
Street art, 31, 44
Style, 12–14, 17, 19, 31, 33, 48, 54, 57, 62, 69, 73, 80, 97
*Style Wars*, 31, 33, 54
Subculture, 36–40, 84, 111
Subway, 2–4, 9–34, 35, 36, 40–45, 47, 49, 53, 54, 57, 58, 64, 80, 92, 93, 98, 99, 128
*Subway Art*, 17, 18, 31, 33, 54
Surveillance, 20, 25, 57, 93, 94, 115
Symbol, 27
Symbolic, 74
Symbolization, 85, 90

## T

Tag, 12, 13, 19, 39, 47, 89, 112
Technological solutions, 41
Technology, 19–22, 93–96
Technology fetishism, 93–96
Terrorism, 99
Theft, 37–38, 92
Thermal-imaging, 94
3D, 15, 17
Throw-up, 10–19, 22, 35, 43, 130
*Time Magazine*, 72, 99–100
Tolerance, 7, 41, 62, 85
Top to bottom, 55n56
Tourism, 119
Tradition, 35, 37, 38, 40, 42, 55, 80, 113
Train, 2, 9, 11, 12, 15, 19, 21–23, 25–27, 29, 31, 34, 35–60, 62, 64, 68, 69, 75, 80, 93, 99, 128
Trickle-down, 117

## U

UGA, 29
Underemployment, 109
Unemployment, 23
Urban, 2–6, 10, 24, 59, 67, 72, 86, 90, 91, 100, 104, 105, 109, 112, 113, 115, 116–124, 129–131
Urban environment, 2, 6, 24, 59, 86, 91, 100, 117, 123, 130
Use-value, 6, 116
US (and/or United States), 1, 2, 23, 33, 42, 72, 94, 129

## V

Vandalism, 42, 44, 51–54, 95, 99
Vandals, 86, 87, 96
Vandal Squad, 21, 94, 96
Video games, 73
Violence, 57–59, 60, 89, 107
Virtue, 38, 119
Visual, 17, 24, 25, 30, 33, 34, 36, 42, 47, 67, 68, 78, 86, 98, 123
Vocabulary, 31, 55

## W

War, 9, 19–29, 34, 62, 93, 109, 112, 113, 114
War on graffiti, 20, 23, 34, 112–114
Western philosophy, 85
Wheat-paste, 44
Whole car, 19
Whole train, 43
*Wild Style*, 14, 15, 31, 54
Writing career, 17
Writing culture, 1, 2, 3, 5, 9–12, 14, 16, 19–22, 28, 30–36, 38–43, 45, 55–60, 61–81, 83, 84, 87, 88, 89, 96, 98, 109, 127–131

## Y

Yards, 4, 12, 20, 21, 25, 31, 36, 42, 43, 57
Youth, 1, 12, 23, 50, 88, 128

## Z

Zero-tolerance, 41

Printed in the United States
By Bookmasters